PCs
Simplified®

Visual

by Elaine Marmel

WILEY

Wiley Publishing, Inc.

PCS SIMPLIFIED®

Published by
Wiley Publishing, Inc.
10475 Crosspoint Boulevard
Indianapolis, IN 46256

www.wiley.com

Published simultaneously in Canada

Library of Congress Control Number: 2010941215

ISBN: 978-0-470-88847-6

Manufactured in the United States of America

10 9 8 7 6 5 4 3 2 1

Trademark Acknowledgments

Contact Us

For general information on our other products and services please contact our Customer Care Department within the U.S. at 877-762-2974, outside the U.S. at 317-572-3993 or fax 317-572-4002.

For technical support please visit www.wiley.com/techsupport.

Wiley Publishing, Inc.

Sales

Contact Wiley
at (877) 762-2974 or
fax (317) 572-4002.

Credits

Acquisitions Editor
Aaron Black

Project Editor
Terri Edwards

Technical Editor
Diane Koers

Copy Editor
Scott Tullis

Editorial Director
Robyn Siesky

Editorial Manager
Rosemarie Graham

Business Manager
Amy Knies

Senior Marketing Manager
Sandy Smith

Vice President and Executive Group Publisher
Richard Swadley

Vice President and Executive Publisher
Barry Pruett

Project Coordinator
Patrick Redmond

Graphics and Production Specialist
Andrea Hornberger

Quality Control Technician
Lauren Mandelbaum

Proofreading
Henry Lazarek

Indexing
Potomac Indexing, LLC

Illustrators
Ronda David-Burroughs
Cheryl Grubbs
Mark Pinto

Screen Artist
Ana Carrillo

About the Author

Elaine Marmel is President of Marmel Enterprises, LLC, an organization which specializes in technical writing and software training. Elaine spends most of her time writing; she has authored and coauthored over 50 books about Microsoft Project, Microsoft Excel, Microsoft Word for Windows, QuickBooks, Peachtree, Quicken for Windows, Quicken for DOS, Microsoft Word for the Mac, Microsoft Windows, 1-2-3 for Windows, and Lotus Notes. From 1994 to 2006, she also was the contributing editor to monthly publications *Inside Timeslips*, *Inside Peachtree*, and *Inside QuickBooks*.

Elaine left her native Chicago for the warmer climes of Arizona (by way of Cincinnati, OH; Jerusalem, Israel; Ithaca, NY; Washington, DC, and Tampa, FL) where she basks in the sun with her PC, her cross-stitch projects, her dog, Josh, and her cats, Watson and Buddy. For many years, she sang barbershop harmony with two International Championship choruses.

Author's Acknowledgments

Nobody writes a book alone; every book is the combined effort of many people. I'd like to thank Jody Lefevere and Aaron Black for giving me the opportunity to write this book; Terri Edwards for managing the book project process efficiently and effectively; Scott Tullis for making me look good; and Diane Koers for her keen eye in keeping me technically accurate. A very special thanks goes to Rob Sheppard (www.robsheppardphoto.com) and Brad Carson (www.bacimages.com) for the beautiful photos they took for this book. Thanks also to the graphics and production teams who labor tirelessly behind the scenes to create the elegant appearance of this book.

How to Use This Book

Who This Book Is For

This book is for the reader who has never used this particular technology or software application. It is also for readers who want to expand their knowledge.

The Conventions in This Book

❶ Steps

This book uses a step-by-step format to guide you easily through each task. Numbered steps are actions you must do; bulleted steps clarify a point, step, or optional feature; and indented steps give you the result.

❷ Notes

Notes give additional information — special conditions that may occur during an operation, a situation that you want to avoid, or a cross reference to a related area of the book.

❸ Icons and Buttons

Icons and buttons show you exactly what you need to click to perform a step.

❹ Simplify It

Simplify It sections offer additional information, including warnings and shortcuts.

❺ Bold

Bold type shows command names, options, and text or numbers you must type.

❻ Italics

Italic type introduces and defines a new term.

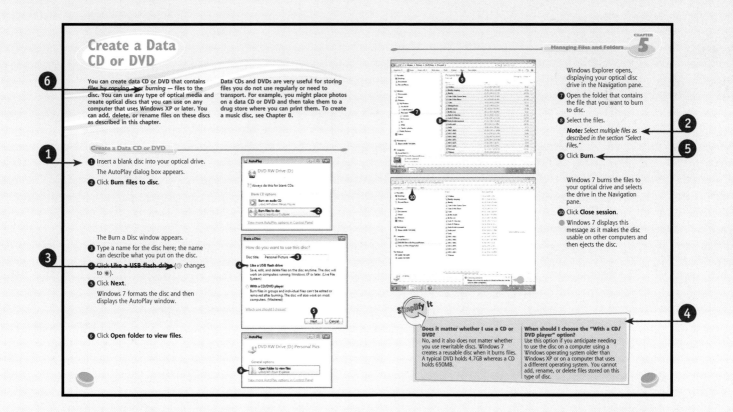

Table of Contents

1

Getting Familiar with Computer Basics

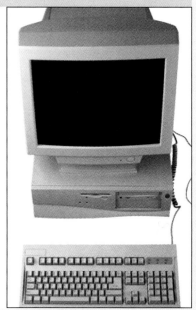

2

Purchasing a Computer

3

Getting Started with Your Computer

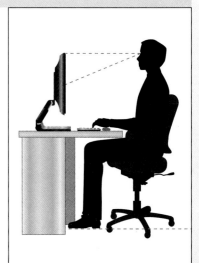

4

Learning Windows 7 Basics

Table of Contents

7

Working with Software

8

Using Multimedia

Table of Contents

9

Working with Portable Computers and Devices

10

Surfing the World Wide Web

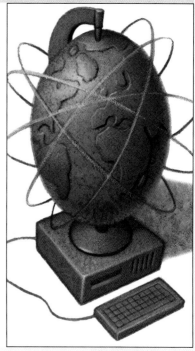

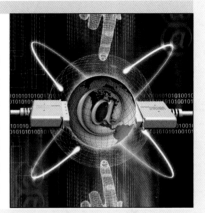

Chapter 1

Getting Familiar with Computer Basics

In this chapter, you read about the benefits computers provide and the ways in which you can use a computer. This chapter describes the different types of computers available in the marketplace, and you take a tour of a typical personal computer. You learn about computer hardware and computer software and the

difference between them along with the devices you can use to provide data to your computer — called *input devices* — and the devices you can use to get data from your computer — called *output devices*. You also learn about the software and hardware brains of your system, memory, and storage.

Discover the Computer

A computer is a device that you can use to store and display text, numbers, images, and sounds, and automate many functions in your daily life. Calculators — calculating machines — were the first electronic computing devices. In the 1940s, the first computers, which filled rooms, added the elements of conditional response and larger memory, enabling us to move beyond numeric computation to automate processes, electronic communications, equipment control, entertainment, education, and more. Over time, computers have evolved to meet our needs, each generation becoming smaller and simultaneously more sophisticated and powerful than its predecessor.

Computer

A *computer* is an electronic device designed to work with information. The computer takes information in, processes that information, and then displays the results. The first computers, developed in the 1940s, filled rooms and were used primarily in military applications. Although computers are similar to calculators, even the smallest computer is more versatile than the most powerful calculator because a computer can do more than mathematical calculations. For example, your computer can take raw sales figures and create a chart.

The Evolution of the Computer

The first computers were large devices, made up of millions of vacuum tubes. With the invention of the transistor in 1947 and the integrated circuit in 1959, and the development of the silicon chip composed of thousands of integrated circuits in the 1970s, computers began to decrease in size. As companies became efficient at producing computer parts, costs began to drop, making mainframe computers affordable for large corporations. The first computers small enough to sit on a desk appeared in the 1970s, became affordable in the 1980s, and continue even today to drop in both price and size.

Personal Computer

A *personal computer* is a small, relatively inexpensive computer designed for use by one person at a time, and enables you to perform tasks such as creating documents, communicating with other people, and playing games. The abbreviation *PC* is most often used to refer to computers that run the Microsoft Windows operating system, as well as to differentiate them from Macintosh computers.

Benefits of Using a Computer

A computer is a powerful and useful tool because it gives you a number of benefits. For example, using a computer, you can quickly perform a job that, without a computer, would take many hours of work. Today's computer-related tools — both hardware and software — help you produce work that looks professional without the cost of hiring a professional. Finally, using a computer enables you to grow as a person; you can learn new skills that are an integral part of today's technological world and, if appropriate, make yourself more marketable in the workplace.

Speed

Computers allow you to perform many everyday tasks more quickly because a computer operates at amazingly fast speeds, typically processing approximately 150 billion operations in 15 seconds. For example, if you manually compose a newsletter, it may take you a week, whereas using a computer, it may take just an afternoon. Or, if you mail a letter to a friend, he or she may receive it in a few days. However, if you send an e-mail, your friend receives it in a few minutes.

Quality

The tools that come with a computer enable you to create high-quality documents that include drawings and photos, even if you are not a typesetter, artist, or an accomplished photographer. With just a few simple techniques, you can create documents that look professional or are exactly suited to your present task.

New Skills

Because we live in a computer age, you often require basic computer skills to accomplish many daily tasks. Typing on a keyboard, using a mouse, and other basic computer skills are useful in many different situations and are often required by employers.

What You Can Do with a Computer

Most electronic devices — calculators, DVD players, camcorders, personal stereos, and so on — do only one thing. However, because computers are versatile by design, they enable you to do many things. For example, you can use a computer to listen to music, watch movies, create flyers, research your family history, educate your children, and play games.

Computers, unlike other electronic devices, can respond to information you provide, therefore producing results that depend on the information you make available. Some people believe that computers simulate a form of intelligence because they respond to information as if it were a stimulus.

Create Documents

You can use your computer to create letters, resumes, memos, reports, newsletters, brochures, business cards, menus, flyers, invitations, and certificates. Anything that you use to communicate on paper, you can create using your computer.

Monitor Your Finances

You can use your computer to perform basic financial management. For example, you can create a budget, record expenses, balance your checkbook, calculate your taxes, and monitor your mortgage. If you run a small business, you can allocate income and expenses, create financial reports, and calculate your profit and loss.

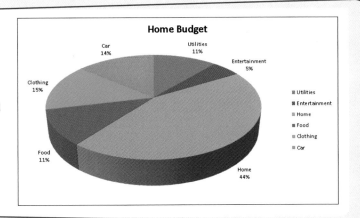

Home Budget

- Car 14%
- Utilities 11%
- Entertainment 5%
- Clothing 15%
- Food 11%
- Home 44%

Legend:
- Utilities
- Entertainment
- Home
- Food
- Clothing
- Car

Perform Research

You can use your computer and the Internet to research almost any topic that you can think of. For example, you can learn more about a vacation destination, trace your family history, access back issues of newspapers and magazines, and compare products before you buy them.

Work with Numbers

You can use a spreadsheet program to work with numbers on your computer. For example, you can create a mortgage amortization schedule, calculate how much money you need to save for retirement, monitor an investment portfolio, and create a business plan.

Store Data

You can use your computer, and the appropriate software, to store and work with large amounts of data. You can track personal items such as pictures, music, recipes, contact information for friends and relatives, and hobbies. For business, you can track contact information for clients and potential clients, product inventory, orders, and bills.

Schedule Your Time

You can use your computer as an electronic day-timer where you track the things you need to do — your "to-do list" — and store upcoming activities, birthdays, anniversaries, events, meetings, and appointments. You can also set up some scheduling programs to remind you of approaching events so that you do not forget them.

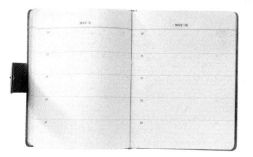

Teach Your Children

You can use your computer to help educate your children. There are many programs available designed to assist children with a plethora of topics. For example, you can find programs that help children learn to read; study math, history, geography, and science; solve problems; learn to draw; and enhance creativity.

continued

What You Can Do with a Computer (*continued*)

Learn New Life Skills

You can use your computer to learn new life skills. Programs are available that teach you how to type, speak a different language, play chess, cook, garden, design a home, play a musical instrument, design and make clothes, and do just about anything you can imagine.

Make New Friends

Using your computer and the Internet, you can enhance your social life. You can find support groups, clubs related to your interests, and organizations that fill needs in your area, and many of these groups have mailing lists you can join. You also can chat electronically with other people by typing messages to them in Internet chat rooms or on Internet forums. You can even join social media sites like Facebook or Twitter or find a date at sites like eHarmony or Match.

Keep in Touch

You can use your computer to communicate with friends, family, colleagues, and clients that you do not often see face to face. You can send e-mail messages and instant messages, and you can even talk to another person using a microphone and your computer's speakers. You also can subscribe to *voice over Internet protocol* (VOIP) providers such as Vonage or Magic Jack and make telephone calls, both local and long distance, using your computer's Internet connection.

Buy and Sell

You can use your computer and the Internet to buy and sell things. Many online stores enable you to purchase anything, from books to baby accessories, and have it delivered to your door. You can even purchase medications for yourself or your pets if you mail the prescription or your doctor faxes it. There are also auction sites, such as eBay, that enable you to sell items that you create or that you no longer need.

Create Items

You can use your computer to bring out your creative side. For example, you can create your own greeting cards or wedding invitations, draw pictures, manipulate digital photos, edit digital movies, record sounds, and compose music. Many artists create prints on their computers.

Play Media

You can use your computer to play digital media, including music CDs, audio files, video files, animations, and DVDs. You also can play movies that you have downloaded from the Internet and music you have downloaded from the Internet or transferred from a music CD to your computer.

Play Games

You can use your computer to play many different types of games. You can solve a puzzle, fly a plane, race a car, go on an adventure, play football or baseball, battle aliens, plan a city, play backgammon or checkers, or deal poker.

Types of Computers

Before you select a computer, you should consider what purpose it will serve in your home or business. For example, if you always use your computer in only one location, a desktop model might work best for you. On the other hand, if you travel frequently and need a computer while you travel, consider a mobile device; depending on your needs, you might want a notebook, netbook, tablet PC, or handheld device.

Many people have more than one computer to fill different needs; for example, you might have a desktop where you perform the bulk of your work and a mobile device.

Tower

Also called a *minitower*, this type of computer system is, by far, the most common type of computer. This type of computer typically comes with a separate computer case, keyboard, and mouse, and many vendors bundle a monitor with the system or permit you to buy the monitor separately. The computer case of a tower system is a vertical box that you stand on the floor.

Desktop

The *desktop* system is still available but not as common as the tower computer. The desktop system also comes with a separate computer case, keyboard, and mouse and an optional monitor. In the desktop system, the computer case lies flat on the desk with the monitor sitting on top.

Notebook

A *notebook* is a computer that combines the case, monitor, keyboard, and mouse in one unit. It is also called a *laptop* or a *portable*. Notebooks are light — usually only four to six pounds — and so you can easily take them out of your office or home. Most notebooks are just as powerful as a desktop system.

Netbook

A netbook is a scaled-down version of a notebook computer. The netbook is physically smaller and typically weighs around two pounds, making it very portable. It stores less data than a notebook, making it a little less powerful than a notebook. Most people who use a netbook as a second computer want only to surf the Internet and collect e-mail when they travel and perhaps take notes at a meeting.

Handheld Device

A handheld device is a very small computer — usually weighing less than a pound — that gets its name because you can hold it comfortably in your hand or carry it in a jacket pocket. In the 1990s, you could buy a handheld device called a *personal digital assistant* (PDA); the most popular one was the Palm Pilot. Today, the functions of the PDA have been incorporated in smartphones like the BlackBerry. Using these devices, you can store your schedule, track mileage, surf the Internet, and check e-mail, among other things.

Server

A *server* is a powerful computer that acts as a central resource for a number of other computers connected to it. These other computers can be PCs or stripped-down *terminals* that use the server to run programs and store data but cannot function on their own like PCs can. Some servers are *mainframes*, which are giant computers that run large-scale operations, such as airline reservation systems.

Tour the Personal Computer

Learning to use a personal computer is much easier if you know what a typical computer looks like and what each major part does. The personal computer requires four major physical components to operate: the computer case and its contents, the monitor, the keyboard, and the mouse.

Computer Case

The *computer case*, also called the *system unit* or *tower*, holds the electronic chips and components that make the computer work. The outside of the case has an on/off switch, and you plug external components primarily into the rear of the case.

Monitor

The *monitor*, also called the *screen* or *display*, is a TV-like component that the computer uses to present text, images, and other information.

Keyboard

The *keyboard* is a typewriter-like device that you use to type information and enter instructions for the computer to follow. To learn how to work the keyboard, see Chapter 3.

Mouse

The *mouse* is a hand-operated pointing device that you use to select and move items on the screen as well as provide instructions for the computer to follow. To learn how to operate the mouse, see Chapter 3.

Personal Computer Accessories

Most people use personal computers with a number of accessory components, also called *peripherals*, such as a printer to produce paper copies of information on the computer or speakers to hear music or video sounds.

Printer

A *printer* is a device that you use to print a document from a computer. Some printers are all-in-one devices that can also fax, copy, and scan documents.

Uninterruptible Power Supply

An *uninterruptible power supply* (UPS) is a device that provides temporary power to your computer should the electricity fail. This device gives you a few minutes to save your work and shut down your computer properly.

Modem

The *modem* is the device that connects your computer to the Internet, through telephone lines, TV cable, or satellite. Some modems, called internal modems, reside inside the computer case, but most are external devices.

Surge Protector

A *surge protector* is a device that protects your computer from damage caused by power fluctuations such as brownouts.

Game Controller

A *game controller* is a device that you can use to the control the action in a computer game.

Speakers

Speakers are devices from which you hear the sound effects, music, narration, and other audio content that your computer generates. You can also use headphones so that only you can hear the audio content.

continued

Tour the Personal Computer *(continued)*

Computer Case Front

The front of the computer case contains a number of buttons and indicator lights, and might also contain a number of holes and slots, called *ports*, into which you plug computer accessory components. Most of the ports appear on the rear of the computer case.

Optical Drive

An *optical drive* is a device that typically reads CDs (compact discs) and DVDs, which resemble musical CDs. Most optical drives can also store information on data CDs and DVDs.

Microphone Port

You can plug a microphone into the *microphone port* that you can use to record and save sound files.

Headphone Port

You can plug in a set of headphones using the *headphone port*. The sound from your computers will come through the headphones instead of through your computer's speakers and avoid disturbing others in the room.

USB Ports

You use a *Universal Serial Bus* (USB) *port* to plug in a USB device such as an external hard drive or a memory card reader. USB ports appear on both the front and the back of the computer.

Power Switch

When the computer is off, press the *power switch* to turn the computer on. Although you can press the power switch to turn off your computer, you should use this method only if your computer freezes. Instead, to turn off your computer, use Windows techniques; see Chapter 3 for details.

Computer Case Rear

The rear of the computer case includes many ports.

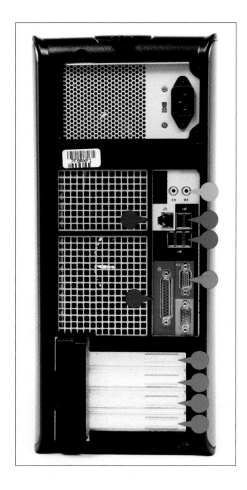

Sound Ports

You use the *sound ports* to plug in sound devices, such as your speakers (the green port on most systems) and microphone (the pink port). Some systems have Line In and Line Out ports to connect the computer to external audio equipment.

Network Port

You use the *network port* to plug in a cable that connects to a network or to a high-speed Internet modem. This is also called an *Ethernet port*.

USB Ports

You use a *Universal Serial Bus* (USB) *port* to plug in a USB device. You use any available USB port to plug in your keyboard and your mouse. Many computer peripherals — including printers and memory card readers — come in USB versions that you plug into any available USB port.

Monitor Port

You use the *monitor port* to plug in the monitor.

LPT Port

You use an *LPT port* to plug a printer in to your computer; many older printers use an LPT port, whereas newer printers use USB ports.

Expansion Slot

You use an *expansion slot* to add an internal computer accessory to your computer. For example, you can use expansion slots to add a TV Tuner card containing TV Tuner Ports or to add an internal modem if you use a dialup Internet connection.

Learn About Computer Hardware and Software

Your introduction to computer basics would not be complete without an explanation of two commonly used terms: *hardware* (or *computer hardware*) and *software* (or *computer software*). These generic terms are used to refer in a global way to the two major categories of components required to make any computer system functional. In the section "Tour the Personal Computer" you read that the personal computer requires, at a minimum, four major physical components to operate: the computer case and its contents, the monitor, the keyboard, and the mouse, all of which are hardware. In addition to these four physical components, any personal computer system also requires software.

What Is Hardware?

Computer hardware consists of the physical components of your computer: the parts, devices, buttons, and ports that you can touch and physically manipulate. Computer hardware comes in two basic varieties: internal and external. You saw a detailed description of both kinds of hardware in the section "Tour the Personal Computer."

Internal Hardware

Internal hardware refers to physical components that reside inside the computer case. These include the *central processing unit* (CPU), which is the hardware brain of the computer, *memory chips* that the computer uses for temporary data storage while you work, *disk drives* that the computer uses for long-term storage, and *circuit boards* — often called *cards* or *adaptors* — which are thin plates on which chips and other electronic components are placed. These cards supply many of the ports on the back of the computer case.

External Hardware

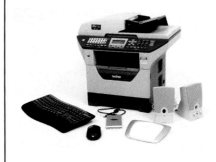

External hardware — also called *peripherals* — refers to components that connect to the computer using ports on the computer case. The monitor, keyboard, and mouse are the most common external hardware devices. The printer and speakers are also popular peripherals. In some cases, you need to add a card inside the computer — an internal piece of hardware — to make available the ports you need to connect an external component. For example, to connect a Media Center PC to a TV, you need to insert a TV Tuner Card inside the computer to make available the TV Tuner ports.

What Is Software?

Unlike computer hardware, computer software is not physical in nature; you cannot touch it or see it, even though it often comes on CDs or DVDs. Computer software, in the form of programs, provides the instructions that enable the computer hardware to perform its tasks. Without software, your monitor would not display anything, your speakers would remain silent, and typing on the keyboard keys would have no effect. Computer software comes in two basic categories: application and system.

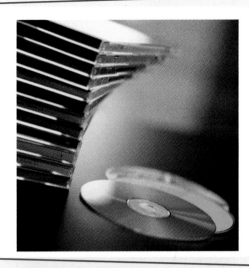

Application Software

Application software refers to the programs that you use to perform specific computer tasks. For example, you can use a spreadsheet program to manipulate numbers. Or, you can use a word-processing program to create documents such as memos and letters. Using a graphics program, you can draw an image, and using a personal financial management program, you can pay bills and manage bank accounts. You use an e-mail program to send and receive e-mail messages.

System Software

System software, more commonly called the *operating system,* serves as the software brain of your computer. The operating system behaves much like a policeman who directs traffic, deciding which programs have the "right of way" to complete their tasks at any given moment, ensuring that no two programs crash into each other so that your computer system continues to function properly. In the world of PCs the most commonly used operating system is Windows 7. You can read more about Windows 7 in Chapters 4 to 7 and periodically throughout the rest of this book.

Get to Know Data Input Devices

The process of entering information into your computer is known as *data input*. In most cases, before you can get information out of your computer, you must put that information into the computer so that the computer can process it. The information you enter consists of either instructions for the computer or data that you want to store on the computer. You can use a variety of devices to enter information into the computer, and this section introduces you to the main types of computer input devices.

Document Scanner

A *document scanner* processes a document or photo much like a photocopy machine processes a document, except that the scanner creates a digital version of the scanned document and sends it to the computer instead of producing a paper copy.

Microphone

Using a *microphone*, you can provide verbal instructions for the computer to follow, or you can record a narration on the computer.

Game Controller

A *game controller*, also called a *joystick*, is a device that you can use to control the action in a computer game. You also can use the joystick to provide instructions to the computer game, such as level and tool selection.

Keyboard

The *keyboard* is a typewriter-like device that you use to provide information to your computer. When you press a key on your keyboard, a signal travels to your computer that identifies that key. Depending on the key that you press, the operating system either displays a character or processes an instruction.

Mouse

The *mouse* is a hand-operated pointing device that you use to select and move items on the screen as well as to provide instructions for the computer to follow. When you move the mouse or press a mouse button, your action sends a signal from the mouse to the computer and the operating system reacts accordingly.

Digital Camera

A *digital camera* takes pictures and stores them in digital form on a memory card in the camera. You can then connect the camera to a computer and move the pictures from the camera to the computer.

Webcam

A *webcam* is a digital camera attached to your computer that takes a series of pictures of a live scene and transfers them to another location. Originally, webcams were used to upload pictures to a Web site, providing effectively a live broadcast. More recently, webcams have come to be used to video-conference.

Get Acquainted with Data Output Devices

As you work on your computer, you send an instruction to obtain a response. The way in which the computer responds — and where the information appears — depends on the request you made.

The process of getting information from your computer is often referred to as *data output*. Your computer can supply information using a number of devices, and this section introduces the main types. Often, the computer's response occurs automatically. For example, when you turn on your computer, the output appears on the monitor. You also can control the computer's response by making certain requests; for example, you can print information.

Display on Monitor

Your monitor is your computer's most important output device. What you see on the screen is a reflection of what is happening inside the computer, and your programs display elements on the screen that enable you to control how the programs work. The monitor also displays what you type, as well as your mouse movements.

Print to Printer

When you finish working with a document, you may want another person to view it. You can print the document on paper using your printer, and then give the resulting document to the other person. The printer converts digital information into words on paper and is the only way you can transfer information from your computer to paper.

Copy to Disk

You can make a copy of a document and store it on media such as a CD or DVD disc, a USB flash drive, an external hard drive, or a memory card. Using these devices, you can make backup digital copies of important documents or share data with another person. For more information, see the section "Learn About Data Storage."

Play on Speakers

Your computer uses speakers to deliver sound. These speakers may be separate units, built into the monitor, or inside the computer case. If the system has an important message to display, the speakers may sound an alert to get your attention. You can use your speakers to play sound files, music CDs, and other audio data.

Learn About the Operating System

The operating system is the software brain of your computer; effectively, it controls the overall operation of your computer. You can compare the purpose and functions of the operating system to a policeman who directs traffic during rush hour. The operating system controls computer startup, application and hardware management, and computer shutdown. Everything that happens on your computer is initiated, processed, and approved by the operating system, and so it is important that you understand how this critical software works. Windows 7 is the most widely used operating system on personal computers.

Startup

When you turn on your computer, the operating system assumes control and prepares the computer for use. For example, it checks for the presence of devices such as the hard drive and your computer's memory, and it runs various checks to ensure that the hardware is functioning properly. The operating system then displays the *interface*, the term used to describe the screen elements that you use to interact with your computer.

Files

One of the main functions of the operating system is to manage a computer's files. A file is an electronic collection of data and instructions that your computer stores as a unit. Your computer contains files that your programs use internally, as well as the documents, images, spreadsheets, and other data that you create. The operating system manages the organization of files so that the computer can produce them upon request.

Device Drivers

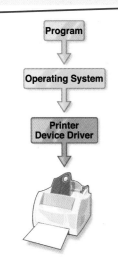

The operating system uses small programs called *device drivers* to communicate with your computer's hardware. For example, when you hook up a printer, a device driver is installed that describes the functioning of the printer to the operating system so that the operating system knows how to send output to the printer. Or, if you insert a CD, DVD, or USB flash drive, the operating system launches a device driver to read and display the contents of the disc.

Programs

The operating system interacts with your application software. For example, when you give the instruction to start a program, the operating system finds the appropriate files and opens them. The operating system also allocates computer resources, such as memory, to your programs.

Data Input

When you press a key on your keyboard, move your mouse, use a game controller, talk into your microphone, or start to scan a document, the operating system intercepts the input, analyzes it, and then directs the input appropriately. For example, as appropriate, the operating system relays an instruction to a program or displays a typed character on the screen.

Data Output

When you request data output, the operating system responds to your request. For example, if you instruct a program to print a document, the operating system sends the document to the printer. Or, when you copy a file to a USB flash drive, the operating system coordinates the action between the computer hard drive and the USB flash drive.

32-bit versus 64-bit

Most new computers today are "64-bit capable," which means that the front side bus, which you will read about in the section "Tour the Central Processing Unit," is 64 bits wide. Older computers have 32-bit buses. Effectively, a system with a 64-bit bus can take advantage of more memory — and therefore has the potential to process information faster — than a system with a 32-bit bus. If your system has a 64-bit bus, you can use a 32-bit or a 64-bit version of the operating system; the 32-bit version recognizes only 4GB of memory, even if your system has more. This important distinction matters to you only if you plan to process lots of graphics or calculations.

Tour the Central Processing Unit

The central processing unit (CPU) is the hardware brain of your computer and, as a result, is the computer's most important component. It handles or directs most of the tasks that occur inside the computer. The CPU is also called the *microprocessor* or *processor*.

Initially, CPUs were designed for single purposes, but this approach was costly, so manufacturers began to standardize the design and mass-produce CPU chips that could be used for many purposes. The invention of the integrated circuit encouraged both standardization and miniaturization so the CPUs no longer appear only in personal computers, but in all kinds of electronics, including cell phones, cars, and kitchen appliances.

What Is a CPU?

Attached to the motherboard, the CPU is a *computer chip*, which is a piece of silicon that contains small electronic devices called *transistors*. These transistors contain components just .09 microns wide (an average human hair is 100 microns wide). The latest personal computer CPUs contain over 100 million transistors and can perform billions of instructions per second.

What Is a Motherboard?

A *motherboard* is the principal circuit board in your computer. It contains connectors for all of the other circuit boards — also called *chips* — that you attach to the computer. Every PC motherboard has a connector to hold the CPU chip as well as connectors to attach disk drives, memory, and circuit boards that enable you to connect your monitor, printer, and other devices to your computer.

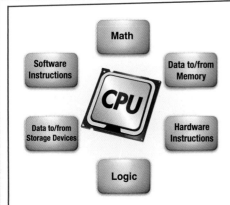

What Is the Function of a CPU?

The purpose of the CPU is to coordinate the flow of data throughout the computer; this is why the CPU is often called the computer's hardware brain. The CPU also performs math and logic calculations, sends data to and retrieves data from memory and storage devices, and processes hardware and software instructions.

CPU Manufacturers

The biggest manufacturer of CPUs is Intel, which makes the Core, Pentium, and Celeron processors for desktop PCs. The other major CPU maker is AMD, which manufactures the Phenom, Athlon, and Sempron chips for desktop PCs. Each family of processor chips by each manufacturer is intended to support different intensities of work on a computer.

CPU Speed

The most common measure of a CPU is its speed. The speed is measured in cycles per second (hertz, or Hz) where a cycle represents a single task performed by the CPU, such as adding two numbers. CPU speeds are usually measured in gigahertz (GHz), or billions of cycles per second.

CPU Caches

Many CPUs come with a feature called a *cache*, which is a storage area where the CPU keeps frequently used data. This feature saves the CPU from having to extract that data from some more distant location in the computer's memory, thus improving computer performance. The latest CPUs have both a cache on the chip (usually called an L1 cache) and a cache between the chip and memory (usually called an L2 or L3 cache) for maximum performance.

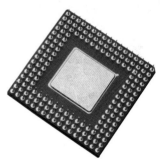

Front Side Bus

The average CPU spends much of its time transferring data to and from the computer's memory. The pathways on which this data travels are collectively called the *front side bus* (FSB), or simply the *bus*. The FSB speed determines how fast data travels between the CPU and memory. As a result, the faster the bus speed (usually measured in MHz [megahertz], or millions of cycles per second), the faster the computer performs. For more information about memory, see the section "Understanding Memory."

Understanding Memory

Memory, stored on a chip inside your computer, is a temporary work area. When you run a program or open a document, the operating system loads the corresponding files from your hard drive into the space provided by memory.

Memory is like a carpenter's workshop: The raw materials are stored in another room (the hard drive) until you need them, and the carpenter brings them into the workshop (memory) when he is ready to use them. When the carpenter has completed the work, the finished piece is moved from the workshop back to storage.

Memory and Performance

Because memory is where the computer holds your running programs and opens documents, the more memory you have, the more programs and documents you can have open. If you want to improve the performance of your computer, you can ask your local computer shop to add more memory to your system. But your operating system puts limits on the amount of memory your computer can use: a 32-bit operating system recognizes only 4GB of memory, whereas a 64-bit operating system recognizes up to 128GB memory.

RAM versus ROM

The memory that a computer uses as a temporary work area is also called *random access memory* (RAM), because the computer can randomly add data to and remove data from this memory. However, keep in mind that the data in RAM is erased when you turn off your computer. In contrast, read-only memory (ROM) stores data permanently, but you cannot change this data. For example, the instructions for initializing your computer's components when you turn on the machine are stored in ROM.

Memory Chip

RAM and ROM are stored on special computer chips called *memory chips*. Each memory chip contains a large number of transistors designed to store computer data.

Memory Module

Computers do not use memory chips individually. Instead, the chips are attached to a special circuit board called a *memory module*. Older computers, built between 1980 and the late 1990s, use a single inline memory module, or SIMM, which holds 9 memory chips on one side of the board. Most computers built after 2000 use a dual inline memory module, or DIMM, which holds 9 memory chips on each side of the board for a total of 18 chips. Adding memory modules can improve the performance and increase the speed of your system within the limitations of your operating system.

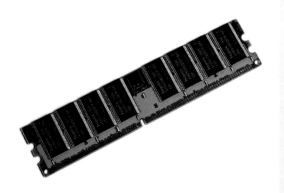

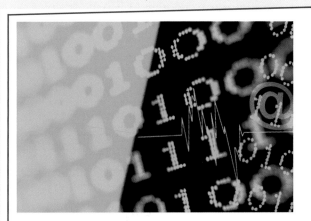

Measure Memory: Bits and Bytes

A memory chip stores data using tiny electronic devices that are either on or off. When the state of a device is on, it has a value of 1, and when the state is off, it has a value of 0. These values are called *bits*, which is short for *binary digit*. Characters, such as letters, numbers, and other symbols, are represented by 8-bit values, which are called *bytes*. For example, the letter *M* is represented by the following byte: 01001101.

Measure Memory: Kilobytes, Megabytes, Gigabytes, and Terabytes

A byte represents a single character of data. Because computers regularly deal with thousands and even millions of characters at a time, a system of measurement is needed to represent these amounts. A kilobyte (KB) represents about 1,000 bytes (equivalent to about a page of text). A megabyte (MB) is about 1,000 kilobytes (equivalent to a thick book), a gigabyte (GB) is about 1,000 megabytes (equivalent to a small library), and a terabyte is about 1,000 gigabytes, or 1 trillion bytes.

Learn About Data Storage

Your computer's memory is only a temporary storage area for data. You can store your data in a more permanent form using one of several different types of storage devices. You can use an internal hard drive or a removable storage device such as an external hard drive or a USB flash drive. You also can use an optical drive to store data.

If you save all of your information only on your computer's internal hard disk and that disk fails, you lose all of your data. Therefore, consider copying the data on the internal hard drive to one of the removable data storage devices.

Hard Drive

The hard drive, also called the *hard disk drive* (HDD) or the *hard disk*, is your computer's main permanent storage area. The hard drive sits inside the computer case and stores your programs and documents. The hard drive is a series of magnetic disks that physically resemble optical discs; like optical discs, the hard drive holds your data even when you turn off your computer. Most current hard drives can store hundreds of gigabytes of data.

Removable Storage

In addition to the hard drive, you can increase your system's storage space using removable media. An external hard drive is generally 6×4×½ inches and attaches to one of the computer's USB ports; you can find drives that hold 1 terabyte of information. You also can use USB flash drives, also called *thumb drives* or *keychain drives* because they are generally about the size of your thumb and some can attach to your keychain. But do not let the size of a USB flash drive fool you; these small devices hold anywhere from 2GB to 64GB of information.

An Overview of Optical Drives

Optical drives (●) are another form of removable storage. The drives themselves are often internally connected to your computer, or you can buy external devices. Regardless of the type of drive — internal or external — the media they use (CDs and DVDs) are removable and portable. As with other technology, optical drives have evolved. Initially, you had to choose between CD and DVD drives and whether the drive could only read discs or both read and write discs. Now, most vendors sell optical drives that work with both CDs and DVDs and can both read and write discs.

Types of Optical Drive Media

A typical CD holds 650MB of information and a typical DVD holds 4.7GB of information. You can buy media that you write to only once or media that you can write to multiple times. The "write-once" media — the CD-R or the DVD-R — is the best choice if you intend to write to the disc on one computer and read it on a different computer. If you intend to use the disc only on one computer, you can safely use rewriteable media — CD-RW or DVD-RW.

Plus or Minus?

In the early days of optical drive development, you had to choose between drives that could only read discs and drives that could both read and write. There was also a period where you could buy a drive that could read and write CDs but only read DVDs. During this period, there was a disc format war going on, reminiscent of the VCR tape format war between Betamax and VHS. Certain optical drives could handle only plus (+) format discs, and other drives could handle only minus (–) format discs. Fortunately, the format wars are over, and today's optical drives can read either format.

Memory Card Reader

With so many different memory card formats available, most memory card readers are multifunction devices that have separate slots for each supported format. You can connect the reader to your computer's USB port and then insert a memory card into the appropriate slot. Many computers now also come with memory card readers built into the front of the case. You find memory cards in devices such as digital cameras, music players, cellular phones, and handheld computers; by inserting the memory card into your computer's memory card reader, you can transfer information.

Other Types of Data Storage

Fading in popularity but still available are floppy disk drives, tape drives, and Zip drives. A floppy drive is a device into which you insert a floppy disk, which is a small (3.5 inches wide) magnetic disk that you can use to read and write data. Because floppy disks hold only 1.44MB of data, most computers now ship without a floppy drive. A tape drive is a device into which you insert a tape cartridge that can store thousands of megabytes. A Zip drive can accept disks that look like floppy disks but hold up to 750MB of data. Large-capacity external hard drives are replacing both tape drives and Zip drives.

Chapter 2

Purchasing a Computer

Before you purchase a computer, you need to know what type of computer is right for you and what extras you really need. This chapter helps you do that by explaining the sales jargon and demystifying the process of buying a computer. You read about selecting a computer type, a CPU, and a version of Windows. You consider how much RAM you need and what kinds of data storage you need. You look at choosing a monitor, video card, and printer, and you consider additional accessory hardware and software. Last, you find tips to consider when making your purchase.

Choose a Computer Type

The most important consideration when purchasing a computer is the type of system that you need. You determine the type of system you need based on what you plan to do with your computer. For example, if you plan to use your computer daily to create documents and perform math, a desktop might be best for you. However, if you need to work on the go, you might consider a notebook, netbook, or tablet PC.

If you need access to e-mail, scheduling, and contact information both in and out of the office, consider a smartphone in addition to any computer you buy.

Desktop

Most computer users buy desktops because these systems offer the most flexible configurations. If your budget is limited, you can purchase a less powerful system with fewer features; if money is not an issue, you can purchase a high-performance computer with many features. If space is an issue, consider an all-in-one, where the contents of the tower — the motherboard containing the CPU chip and all of the ports for peripheral devices — are part of the monitor.

Notebook

Whether you travel for business or just want to work in the local coffee shop for a while, a notebook computer offers the flexibility to work almost anywhere. Generally weighing in the range of 5 to 7 pounds, with screens ranging from approximately 14 to 16 inches, keep in mind that a notebook tends to cost more than the equivalent desktop computer.

Netbook

If your work needs are light while you travel, you might consider a netbook, which contains a smaller hard drive, no optical drive, and is smaller and lighter weight than a notebook. The netbook also offers you wireless access to the Internet. Netbooks generally weigh 1 to 2 pounds and come with 10- or 12-inch screens.

Select a CPU

In computer ads, the CPU is usually the first component mentioned because it is the hardware heart and soul of the computer. So, understanding the features of a CPU is important. You should look at both the CPU type and the CPU speed. The operating system you choose also affects the CPU you need because each operating system has minimum CPU requirements. Finally, you should determine what cache memory is installed on the CPU because the cache memory can affect the performance of the CPU.

CPU Type

If you do not need a powerful computer, look for a system with an Intel Celeron or AMD Sempron processor. For a more powerful computer, look for an Intel Core or Pentium or an AMD Phenom or Athlon processor. Notebooks generally use the same processors as desktop computers, and netbooks, because of their scaled-down size, typically use Intel's Atom processor.

CPU Speed

Generally, the slower the CPU speed, the less expensive and less powerful the computer is. If you want to use your computer for basic activities, such as writing letters or memos, sending e-mails, and surfing the World Wide Web, then you do not need the fastest available processor. Any of today's processors should be fast enough for you.

Minimum CPU Requirements

If you plan to use Windows 7 as your operating system, you need a CPU with a speed of at least 1 gigahertz (GHz) and either a 32-bit or a 64-bit processor. Note that Windows 7 also has minimum RAM and hard disk requirements. See "Choose an Edition of Windows" for details.

Cache Memory

Cache memory can greatly improve the performance of a CPU, although the more memory on the chip, the more expensive a system is. If the advertisement uses only the word *cache*, it usually refers to the L2 cache, although occasionally you see references to the L3 cache. L1 is the smallest and fastest but also the most expensive to expand, so vendors rarely change the size of L1 cache.

Choose an Edition of Windows

Windows 7 comes in four editions: Starter, Home Premium, Professional, and Ultimate. Starter contains the fewest features and Ultimate contains the most. Regardless of the version you buy, all Windows 7 features are available on the disc; the product code you enter when you install Windows determines what edition you install and therefore what features are available.

In addition, in any Windows 7 box, you get two discs: one for 32-bit systems and one for 64-bit systems. You use the disc that works with your system. Without buying additional discs, you can upgrade to a more feature-rich edition by simply buying a product code from Microsoft.

Minimum Computer System Requirements

To use any edition of Windows 7, your computer must have a 1 gigahertz (GHz) or faster 32-bit (x86) or 64-bit (x64) processor. A machine containing a 32-bit processor must also contain at least 1 gigabyte (GB) of RAM, whereas a machine containing a 64-bit processor must contain at least 2GB of RAM. The hard drive of a 32-bit processor system must have 16GB of available space; the 64-bit processor system needs 20GB of available space. Finally, regardless of the processor, the system must have a DirectX 9 graphics device with a Windows Display Driver Model (WDDM) 1.0 or higher driver; most new systems come with these graphics components.

Windows 7 Starter Edition

Of all the editions of Windows 7, the Starter edition is the only one you cannot purchase individually; you find it preinstalled on many netbook computers. This scaled-down edition of Windows 7 enables you to perform everyday productivity tasks such as opening and working in programs, surfing the Internet, and handling e-mail. You have access to Windows Gadgets, and you can play games and use Windows Media Player to watch video clips. You can view available networks and connect to one; you also can join a Homegroup — typically a private network. You cannot customize the Windows desktop, and the Starter edition works only on 32-bit processors.

Windows 7 Home Premium Edition

The Home Premium edition of Windows 7 contains all of the features found in the Starter edition, so you get all of the functionality in the Starter edition plus the ability to customize the desktop and perform other personalization tasks, create a Homegroup, watch Internet TV, play multiplayer games, and use the Windows Media Center to watch movies and live TV. You also get multiple monitor support and Windows 7 Aero features, including Peek and Shake, plus some additional Windows accessory programs.

Windows 7 Professional Edition

The Professional edition of Windows 7 contains all of the features found in the Home Premium edition plus support for joining domains, the ability to function in Windows XP mode and run Windows XP legacy programs, connect to remote desktops, and perform network backups. This edition of Windows 7 is most useful in a business environment.

Windows 7 Ultimate Edition

The Windows 7 Ultimate edition contains all available features in Windows 7; you can think of it as the Cadillac of all Windows 7 editions. In addition to the features found in the Windows 7 Professional edition, Windows 7 Ultimate gives you the ability to install Language Packs so that you can work in multiple languages. It also makes available a variety of tools used by information technology (IT) professionals to manage large-scale network operations. Windows 7 Ultimate is best suited to a large business enterprise environment.

Upgrade to Windows 7

If you have a computer currently running either Windows XP or Windows Vista, you are legally eligible to purchase an upgrade version of Windows 7. When you run the installation, Windows prompts you to choose either Upgrade or Custom. Choosing **Upgrade** enables you to install Windows on top of your current installation, keeping all of your programs and data. You can upgrade from Windows Vista Home Premium to Window 7 Home Premium, from Window Vista Business to Windows 7 Professional, or from Window Vista Ultimate to Windows 7 Ultimate. In all other cases, you must choose **Custom**, which wipes all information off your hard drive before installing Windows.

Windows Easy Transfer Utility

If you need to perform a custom upgrade to Windows 7, you can download this free utility from Microsoft's Web site and let it back up your data to an external hard drive before you upgrade to Windows 7. Then, after you finish installing Windows 7, you can use the same utility to restore your data. The process is simple, and the utility does the work for you; just accept what you see on-screen. After you restore your data, you need to reinstall all the programs you had on your system before you upgraded.

Windows 7 Upgrade Advisor

If you are planning to install Windows 7 on a computer you already use, you can download for free from Microsoft's Web site the Windows 7 Upgrade Advisor. The Windows Upgrade Advisor evaluates your hardware and software and notifies you of anything that will not function under Windows 7.

32 bit versus 64 bit

Whether you upgrade an existing computer or buy a new one with Windows 7, you should make note of whether you are using the 32-bit or the 64-bit version. 32-bit programs run in either version, but 64-bit programs require the 64-bit version.

Determine How Much RAM You Need

The amount of random access memory (RAM) in your computer determines how fast your computer runs and what types of programs you can use. When you consider the amount of RAM to put in your computer, you will find minimum requirements stated for Windows 7, but those minimum requirements do not necessarily address your needs, which depend largely on the type of computing you expect to do. For example, if you intend to run more than one program at a time — and many people do run multiple programs simultaneously without even realizing they are doing so — you need more RAM than the minimum.

Minimum Requirements

The amount of RAM your system needs depends on whether you intend to install the 32-bit or 64-bit version of Windows 7. Start by determining whether you are using a 32-bit processor or a 64-bit processor; if you have a 64-bit processor you can install either version of Windows, whereas a 32-bit processor must use the 32-bit version of Windows. For any edition of Windows 7, from Starter to Ultimate, a machine containing a 32-bit processor must contain at least 1 gigabyte (GB) of RAM, and a machine containing a 64-bit processor must contain at least 2GB of RAM.

Real-World Minimum Requirements

For day-to-day work, the suggested RAM minimums for Windows 7 are too small. For any edition of the Windows 7 operating system, from Starter to Ultimate, a computer with a 32-bit processor performs much better if it has at least 2GB of RAM, and a machine with a 64-bit processor performs much better if it has at least 4GB of RAM.

Multitasking Requirements

On any edition of Windows 7, from Starter to Ultimate, you can run multiple programs at the same time; this capability is referred to as *multitasking*. It is not unusual to simultaneously run programs such as word processing, spreadsheet, and e-mail, and a Web browser; many people run even more programs simultaneously. If you plan to run four or five (or more) programs at the same time, you need more memory in your system beyond the minimum system requirements, and you will probably be happiest with 2GB of RAM on a machine with a 32-bit processor and 4GB on a machine with a 64-bit processor.

Graphics and Database Requirements

If you plan to use programs that manipulate digital photos, edit digital videos, or work with extremely large files such as databases, you need even more RAM. On a machine with a 32-bit processor, you should have 3GB, the maximum that the 32-bit version of Windows 7 recognizes. On a machine with a 64-bit processor, Windows 7 recognizes up to 128GM of RAM, but you can start with 8GB to see how well your system handles your processing.

Select Data Storage Options

When buying a computer, you can make choices about the types of data storage devices you include in the computer and, in some cases, you can make other decisions about a storage device. For example, when choosing a hard drive, you can choose its size and speed, and the speed of a drive is affected by the type of drive you select. You also can decide whether to include an optical drive and a built-in memory card reader or plan to purchase external ones. The decisions that you make are important because they determine how you store data on your computer.

Minimum Hard Drive Size

Windows 7 requires at least 16GB of free space on your hard drive to install, but you need more space to load additional programs and data. Today, the cost of hard drives has come down so much that you can purchase an 80GB hard drive for less than $50, and many vendors offer an upgrade to a 160GB drive — double the size — for an additional $10. You can purchase a 1 terabyte (TB) drive for about $75. With the cost being so low, there really is no reason to limit the size of the hard drive.

Hard Drive Performance

In addition to the size of the hard disk, it is important to consider the hard drive's speed. Traditional hard drives contain platters, and the *rotational speed* refers to how fast the hard drive platters rotate. A low-end hard drive may spin at 5,400 revolutions per minute (RPM), whereas most drives rotate at 7,200; there are high-end drives that rotate at 10,000 RPM or even 12,000 RPM. New solid-state drives do not use mechanical moving parts; instead, they use solid-state memory. Because they do not contain moving parts, they are typically faster than their electromechanical counterparts, but they are also more expensive.

Optical Drive

Most optical drives (●) today both read and write CDs and DVDs; drives that both read and write are sometimes called *burners*. The cost of the optical drive has also dropped dramatically in price to the point where there is no good reason to purchase a drive that works exclusively with CDs or only reads DVDs but does not write them. And some software vendors distribute their software on DVDs, so there is absolutely no reason to look for a drive that reads and writes only CDs.

Memory Card Reader

You can buy a computer that has memory card readers built into the front of the computer case, but the more practical approach is to purchase a memory card reader that attaches to your computer using a USB port. If you use multiple formats of memory cards on a frequent basis, consider purchasing a reader that supports the formats you use.

Choose a Monitor and Video Card

Because you look at the monitor all day long, you should get a good monitor and video card that is easy on your eyes and does not break your budget. You should consider not only the type of monitor but its size and its dot pitch as well. Because the monitor works hand in hand with the video card in your computer, you should pay close attention to the quality of the video card you choose to help ensure that your monitor can do everything you want it to do.

Monitor Type

Although you can still purchase a *cathode ray tube* (CRT), most people prefer the newer *liquid crystal display* (LCD, also called a *flat panel*) type of monitor. An LCD is smaller and sharper than a CRT, and LCD prices have dropped significantly in recent years, so LCDs are now the most popular monitor type by far. You can buy both traditional LCD monitors and wide-screen LCD monitors, which resemble flat-screen TVs. Advanced LCD display technology monitors use an LED backlight that produces brilliant colors but requires less power than a similarly sized standard LCD monitor.

Monitor Size

A large monitor allows you to display more elements on the screen than a small monitor. You can determine the size of a monitor by measuring diagonally from corner to corner. Keep in mind that if you see a computer ad that says "19-inch monitor (18.0-inch viewable image size, or v.i.s.)," this means that although the monitor measures 19 inches diagonally, only 18 inches of that measurement are actually used to display the image.

Video Card

The *video card*, also known as the *graphics card*, is an internal circuit board that generates the images that you see on your monitor. Your main concern when purchasing a graphics card is the amount of *video memory* that it contains. With more video memory, you can set your computer display at a higher resolution to view a crisper image than at a lower resolution, display more colors, and open many large graphics files at once.

Choose a Printer

A printer enables you to create a paper copy of a document or photo stored on your computer. You can choose from a variety of printers with different capabilities to meet your printing requirements. When purchasing a printer, you should consider not only the price, but the print quality and speed of the printer. Also think about whether you need to print in color. Also think about the type of ink the printer uses and research the cost of the different types of inks, because ink will be the long-term cost associated with your printer.

Printer Types

A laser printer uses a laser beam to apply an electrostatic charge to a rotating drum, which then picks up the toner and applies it to the paper; lasers are fast and produce crisp images, and are no longer expensive unless you want a color laser. An inkjet printer outputs text and images by spraying ink on the paper; an inkjet is slower and produces less crisp images than a laser printer, but it offers color output for far less money. A *photo printer* specializes in printing images from a digital camera.

Print Quality and Ink

Print quality, or *resolution*, is measured in dots per inch (dpi): the higher the quality, the sharper and more detailed the printed text or image. A typical laser or inkjet printer is capable of printing at 1,200 dpi, which means that each square inch of print has 1,200 dots across by 1,200 dots down (this is sometimes written as 1,200×1,200 dpi). Laser cartridges have come down in price and generally produce more printed pages per cartridge than inkjet cartridges. Also, most inkjet printers require both a black and at least one color cartridge be installed even if you are printing only in black.

Print Speed

Print speed is measured in pages per minute (ppm). A good laser printer for home or small office use can output pages at about 23 ppm. For inkjets and photo printers, a print speed of about 16 ppm in color and 20 ppm in black is typical.

All-In-One Printers

For a slightly higher price than a stand-alone printer, you can get an all-in-one printer — either inkjet or laser — that also enables you to send and receive faxes, copy documents, and scan documents and photos. Keep in mind that the scanning and copying components have their own resolution values, with higher values giving you better-quality scans and copies.

Add Other Hardware and Software

To complement your basic computer setup, you can add other hardware devices that expand the capabilities of your computer system. For example, you might want to add a network card if you plan to use a high-speed Internet connection or a modem if you plan to use a low-speed Internet connection. And, you might want to consider adding a router to your system to help protect you while connected to the Internet. In addition, your computer's operating system comes with a number of programs. However, many of these programs have only minimal features, and so you may want to upgrade to specialized applications.

Network Card

A network card is a circuit board that enables your computer to join a network, which is a collection of connected computers. You also need a network card if you want to surf the Internet using a high-speed connection. For more information about the Internet, see Chapter 10.

Modem

If you want to establish a connection to the Internet, then you need a modem. Instead of using network cards, older computers used modems that connected the computer to the Internet via telephone line. Today, you use a cable/DSL modem. Cable and DSL are two different methods of connecting to the Internet; cable is generally faster than DSL.

Router

A router is a central connection point for all of the computers on the network that can also route incoming data to a specific network address. This is useful when the computers share a high-speed Internet connection because the router ensures that the Internet data goes to the computer that requested it. The router also contains a hardware firewall that helps protect your computer from attacks on the Internet. You plug your high-speed modem directly into the router, and then plug your computers into the router.

Wireless Connectivity

If you want to connect to the Internet wirelessly or join a wireless network with your desktop, netbook, notebook, or tablet PC, then you need a router that has wireless networking capabilities built in. This feature is usually designated as 802.11b, 802.11g, or 802.11n. Because wireless connections are less secure than wired ones, you also need to implement wireless security. For more information, see Chapter 12.

Audio Accessories

For you to hear the sounds generated by your computer, such as the music from audio CDs, your system needs a circuit board called a *sound card*. Most computers come with sound cards installed and a low-quality speaker. You can upgrade to better sound cards that support Dolby digital sound and other audio features, and you can purchase external speakers and, if you want, a subwoofer for the best audio experience.

Productivity Suite

A *productivity suite* (also called an *office suite*) is a collection of programs that usually includes a word processor, spreadsheet, presentation graphics program, and a database. These programs share a similar interface, making it fast and easy for you to learn each program. The most popular, as well as the most expensive, is Microsoft Office. Less expensive alternatives are Microsoft Works and WordPerfect Office. OpenOffice, a free alternative, is available by downloading from the Internet.

Graphics

If you want to create your own images, you may want to use a different graphics program than the one that ships with your operating system. For example, you can choose graphics software such as Adobe Illustrator. If you want to work with digital photos, consider photo-editing programs such as Adobe Photoshop Elements, Corel Paint Shop Photo Pro, or Windows Live Photo Gallery — free from Windows Live Essentials.

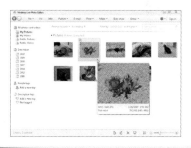

Security

Although your operating system has built-in Internet security, you should supplement with an antivirus program that protects your computer from viruses and other *malware* — software designed to damage your computer. Popular programs are Norton AntiVirus, McAfee AntiVirus, and Eset NOD32 Antivirus. Each of these manufacturers also sells a security suite product that adds a software firewall to your computer, but if you use a router, many users find it less confusing to use the Windows Firewall with an antivirus product.

Tips on Purchase Considerations

Before you purchase a computer, you must consider other factors before making your decision.

Where to Buy

Always purchase your computer from a reputable store or online vendor, such as a well-known chain or smaller outlet that other people have recommended to you. Disreputable retailers abound in the computer business, and so taking a chance simply to save a few dollars is not worth it.

Mail Order or In-Store?

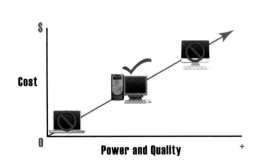

Many first-time computer buyers are concerned about buying online because they fear that they will not get support for the product they purchase. Remember that online retailers do not survive in business if they do not provide support for their products. You can safely buy from an online retailer that has been in business for at least five years.

Price

When buying your first computer, it is a good idea to avoid the low end and the high end of the price range. Low-priced computers are often too slow for day-to-day use, and are made with cheap parts that may not last very long. High-priced computers are usually more powerful than what you need. Mid-priced computers generally have the best combination of quality and performance.

Promotions

You can often save money by watching for special promotions that computer dealers offer. For example, a dealer may offer extra RAM or a DVD burner free with the purchase of a new computer. Similarly, a retailer may include brand-name printers or other peripherals in the purchase at very low prices. However, do not buy a computer because it comes with extra software unless you are familiar with the software. Most users do not use extra software included on PCs they buy, and the extra software ends up slowing down the computer.

Expandability

To get the most out of your computer investment in the long term, you might want to be able to expand the computer's capabilities rather than buy a completely new system. To ensure expandability, look for the computer that has extra slots for memory modules and extra expansion slots for circuit boards. If expandability is your goal, avoid purchasing a computer that uses an ultrasmall form factor case because it lacks these expansion features. Instead, purchase a tower case.

Installation

Many computer dealers offer to install your new system for a fee. However, setting up a basic computer system is easy, and so you may want to save your money and set up the computer yourself. For more information about getting started with your computer, see Chapter 3.

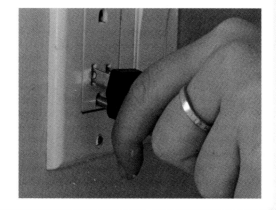

Chapter 3

Getting Started with Your Computer

After you purchase your new computer, you need to set up your work area and connect the computer components. If you are not already familiar with using a computer system, then you should also learn how to use basic devices such as the keyboard, mouse, and CD drive.

Set Up Your Work Area

To ensure your work area is comfortable and you are productive, you should place your computer workstation in a well-lighted, well-ventilated area, select a comfortable chair designed for work at a computer workstation, and properly adjust it. You should also ensure that the computer is located in a low-traffic area.

You also need to properly position your computer and its components. Sitting at the computer, typing, and using the mouse for long periods can cause injuries, including repetitive stress injuries (RSI) such as carpal tunnel syndrome. You can take steps to prevent these injuries.

Select a Suitable Computer Desk

Ensure that your computer desk is sturdy and stable. It should also have a large enough surface area to hold all of the computer's desktop components, as well as any books, papers, and other materials that you may use as you work. If you have the space, consider an L-shaped desk so that you have both a work surface and space for your computer.

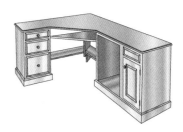

Chair

An uncomfortable or poorly designed chair can affect your work performance and cause you to experience physical problems. You need a chair that has a contoured seat and good lower-back support. It should also have mechanisms to adjust the seat height as well as the angle of both the seat and the back support. Most people find that chairs with arms, particularly adjustable arms, provide the best support and comfort.

Location

Choose a clean, dry, and cool location. It should also be well lit, preferably from above or behind the monitor to prevent glare. Avoid high-traffic areas where people may bump into the computer case and possibly damage the system. Ensure that electrical outlets are nearby, as well as a telephone jack. If you plan to use a high-speed Internet connection, you need a cable outlet nearby; if you do not have one, your cable provider can install one.

Position Components

Position the monitor to maximize work surface for papers. For an L-shaped workstation, place the monitor in the corner of the L. A tower-style computer case goes on the floor, either under or beside the desk. However, if you have a desktop-style computer, put the computer case on the desk and place the monitor on top of it. The keyboard and mouse sit on the desk in front of the monitor. Speakers should also go on the desk; if you have a subwoofer, place it on the floor for the best sound.

Basic Ergonomics

You can apply the principles of ergonomics to design a work area that maximizes your comfort and safety. Sit up straight in your chair with your feet flat on the floor. Adjust the chair height so that your forearms are parallel to the floor when you type, and your eyes are level with the top of your monitor. Place your keyboard and mouse on your desk so that you can comfortably reach them while resting your elbows on the arms of the chair. No part of your forearms should rest on the desk. Remember to take short breaks periodically.

Ergonomic Accessories

There are many accessories that you can buy to ensure good ergonomics. To help keep your wrists straight, you can use wrist rests on both your keyboard and mouse. Many keyboards come with built-in wrist rests and an ergonomic keyboard keeps your hands positioned for the least stress. A trackball mouse significantly reduces the movement — and therefore the stress — of your mouse hand; see Use a Mouse for more information. If you cannot physically position the height of your chair, try using an adjustable keyboard tray and a monitor stand. To keep your feet positioned properly, you can use a footrest.

Connect the Computer Components

You assemble your system by connecting devices to the appropriate ports on the back of the computer case. Some of the devices you plug in require their own electrical power source. After you plug the devices into the computer, you can plug the other end of any device needing power into a surge protector or uninterrupted power supply (UPS).

On most PCs, the ports on the back of the case are color-coded to match the plugs on the accessory devices. In addition, most device plugs fit into only one type of port, so it is not possible to plug a device into the wrong port.

Charge the UPS

An uninterrupted power supply (UPS) provides your computer with limited backup power should the electricity fail. The UPS gives you the opportunity to save your work and shut down your computer correctly in the event of a power failure. To use a UPS effectively, you must charge it for several hours — often overnight — before relying on it.

Unpack the Components

Place the computer boxes on the floor, open them, and remove each component. Double-check with the packing list to ensure that you received everything that you ordered. If the computer arrived on a cold day, give the components a couple of hours to warm up to room temperature. At this stage, do not plug anything into an electrical outlet. If you bought your monitor, printer, and other accessory devices from different suppliers, wait until you have all components before you start connecting components.

Connect the Main Components

Monitor

Your monitor has two cables: a video cable that connects to the computer and a power cord that connects to an electrical power source. The video cable has a D-shaped plug that you can insert into the port with the same shape on the back of the PC. Leave the power cord unplugged for now.

Keyboard and Mouse

Older computers used specialized ports for the keyboard and the mouse, but now the keyboard and mouse connect to your computer using any available USB port. Although your computer comes with USB ports on both the front and the back, save the ones on the front for devices you plug and unplug frequently. Pick any two USB ports on the back of the computer for your keyboard and mouse.

Speakers

The sound ports on the back of the computer are typically color-coded to match the plugs of the sound devices. Connect one speaker — typically color-coded green — to the PC's Line Out jack, and connect the second speaker to the first speaker. Many new computers have headphone and microphone jacks on both the front and back of the computer to enable you to connect these devices when you need them.

Printer

Most newer printers connect via a USB cable, and you can plug the printer's USB cable into any USB port; use one of the ports on the back because you will not plug and unplug the printer on a regular basis. Older printers use cables that have a large connector on one end that fits into the printer and a slightly smaller connector, shaped like an elongated D, on the other end that fits into the PC.

Connect a Cable Modem

For a high-speed Internet connection, use a network cable to connect the cable modem that you purchase or rent from your cable service provider to the Internet port of a router; some routers refer to the Internet port as the Uplink port or the WAN port. Then, use a networking cable to connect the computer's network port to any port on the router except the Internet port. If you choose not to use a router, use a network cable to connect the network port on the back of the computer directly to the cable modem.

Connect the Power Cords

You can now plug the power cords for your computer, monitor, and sound system devices into an uninterrupted power supply (UPS), which protects those devices from electrical damage. Do not plug a laser printer into a UPS or you will void the warranty of the UPS. Instead, plug the laser printer into a surge protector rated 700 joules or higher.

Turn On the Computer for the First Time

Once you have connected your peripherals to your computer, you are ready to start your computer for the first time. If you are using an uninterrupted power supply (UPS), make sure that you plug it in and give it time to charge fully before you turn on anything connected to it.

Before you turn on the computer, turn on any devices connected to it, such as a printer. The first time you turn on your computer, the operating system asks for some standard information from you; after you provide it, the operating system finishes loading and you can begin using your PC.

Check the Charge on Your UPS

Make sure you have charged your UPS before you use anything plugged into it. The display lights on the UPS show you that the UPS is fully charged (●). Once a UPS is fully charged, it provides you with enough battery power to save your work and shut down your computer correctly should the electricity fail. Once you fully charge your UPS, you can leave it on permanently; there is no need to shut it off.

Turn On Your Peripherals

Before you turn on your computer, turn on all of your computer's peripheral devices that have separate on/off switches, such as your monitor, printer, and speakers. Although you may subsequently turn off your computer, you typically leave on the monitor and speakers because they consume almost no power when not in use. If you use a surge protector for a laser printer, you should turn it on.

Turn On Your Computer

Press your computer's power button (●). You should see lights flashing on the computer case and monitor, and information should begin to appear on your monitor. Typically, you initially see the computer vendor's logo on-screen as the computer powers up.

Troubleshoot Power-Up Problems

If nothing happens when you turn on your system, check both the monitor's and the computer's power cord connections at both ends to ensure that you have fully plugged in the cord. Also, check that the UPS or surge protector is plugged in and turned on. Finally, ensure that you have turned on your monitor, and adjust the brightness control to a comfortable level.

Follow Setup Instructions

Each PC manufacturer has its own setup program that runs the first time that you start the computer. This setup finishes the setup of Windows and usually takes just a few minutes. You are typically asked for the following information:

- Your name.
- A name for your computer. Keep the name under 15 characters, do not use only numbers, and do not use spaces or any of the following special characters: < > ; : " * + = \ | ? ,
- The password that you want to use when you log onto Windows. Although the password is optional, using a password helps keep your computer secure; see Chapter 7 for details.
- Your geographic location so that Windows can correctly set the date and time.
- If you have a network card installed in your computer, you are prompted to specify the type of network; choose **Home**.

Wait for the Operating System to Start

After you answer the on-screen questions, Windows loads. The on-screen questions were a "one time only" event; you will not see the questions the next time you turn on your computer. The startup is complete when you see the Windows desktop.

Use a Keyboard

The keyboard is your most important device for sending instructions and data to the computer, and so you should know how to use it. Every computer manufacturer creates a vendor-specific keyboard, and you also can buy third-party keyboards. Although each keyboard performs the same general function, some do more than others. For example, you can purchase keyboards that come with specialized keys that automatically open your Internet browser or your e-mail program or enable you to control multimedia by, for example, raising or lowering volume.

Keep in mind that your keyboard layout may be different from the one shown here.

Specialty/Programmable Keys

Most keyboards from third-party vendors have keys for special tasks, such as opening your Internet browser or playing media. In some cases, you can reprogram these keys to perform other functions.

Function Keys

`F1` through `F12` are most often used as shortcut keys in programs. For example, in most programs, you can press `F1` to display the program's Help system.

Escape

Press `Esc` to stop the current task or when an application does something unexpected on your screen.

Caps Lock

`Caps lock` is a toggle key; press it once to enable the Caps Lock feature and press it again to disable the Caps Lock feature. When you enable the Caps Lock feature, all letters you type appear in uppercase on-screen.

Shift

Press and hold `Shift` to type the uppercase version of any letter you select. Use `Shift` to produce the characters that appear on the number keys above the keyboard letters; for example, press and hold `Shift` and press `4` to produce a dollar sign ($).

Ctrl

You use `Ctrl` (pronounced *control*) in combination with other keys to trigger predefined actions in a program. For example, in most programs, you can press and hold `Ctrl` and press `S` to save your current document.

Windows

Press `⊞` to open the Windows 7 Start menu.

Alt

You use `Alt` in shortcut key combinations to trigger predefined actions in a program. For example, if you press and hold `Alt` as you press `F4` (written in this book as `Alt` + `F4`), you close the current program.

Spacebar

Press `Spacebar` to insert a blank space between letters.

Application

Press `▤` to see the shortcut menu associated with the currently selected item on-screen.

Enter

In a text document, you can press `Enter` to start a new paragraph. In programs other than word processing programs, you can press `Enter` to initiate or complete an action.

Backspace

Press [Backspace] to remove the character immediately to the left of the insertion point.

Delete

Press [Delete] to remove the character immediately to the right of the insertion point.

Navigation Keys

Use the navigation keys to move through a document. Press [Home] to move the insertion point to the beginning of the current line or [End] to move to the end of the line. Press [Pgup] to move up one screen, or [Pgdn] to move down one screen.

Arrow Keys

Use the arrow keys to move the insertion point one character or one line at a time in the direction the arrow key indicates.

Num Lock

Press [Num lock] to enable or disable the numbers on the numeric keypad. When enabled, the keys on the numeric keypad produce numbers. When disabled, the keys on the numeric keypad become the directional navigation keys indicated below the numbers.

Numeric Keypad

The numeric keypad enables you to quickly enter numbers when you press [Num lock] to enable the Num Lock feature.

Use a Mouse

Today's computers are built with the mouse in mind, and so it pays to learn the basic mouse techniques that you will use throughout your computing career: clicking, double-clicking, right-clicking, and dragging — also called *click and drag*. Typically, you click to position the mouse pointer or perform an action, double-click to launch a program, right-click to view a shortcut menu, and click and drag to select text.

If you have never used a mouse before, then you should remember to keep all your mouse movements slow and deliberate while you are learning how to use it. You should also practice the techniques in this section as much as you can.

Use a Mouse

Click the Mouse

① Position the mouse pointer (⮝) over the object you want to work with.

② Click the left mouse button.

● Depending on the object, the operating system either selects the object or performs some action in response to the mouse click, such as displaying the Windows 7 menu.

Double-Click the Mouse

① Position the mouse pointer over the object you want to work with.

② Click the left mouse button twice in quick succession.

● The operating system usually performs some operation in response to the double-click action, such as displaying the Windows Vista Recycle Bin window.

● Click the **Close** button (❎) to close this window.

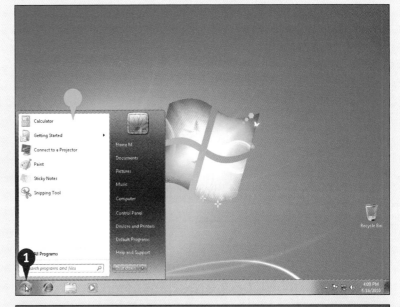

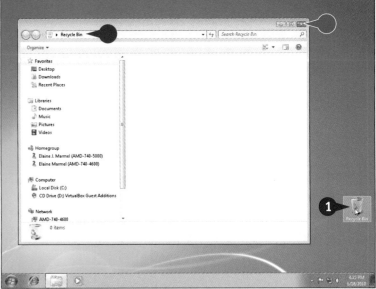

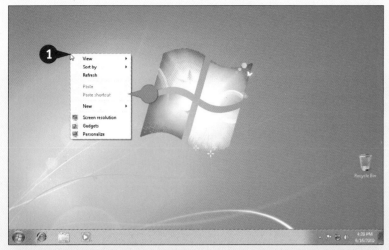

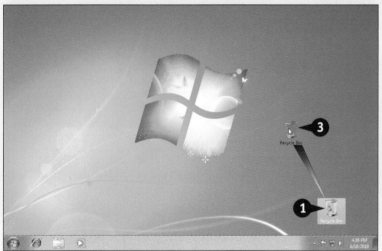

Right-Click the Mouse

1 Position ⌖ over the object with which you want to work.

2 Click the right mouse button.

● The operating system displays a shortcut menu when you right-click an object.

Note: *The contents of the shortcut menu depend on the object that you right-clicked.*

You can click a command on the menu or click outside the menu to close it.

Click and Drag the Mouse

1 Position ⌖ over the object you want to work with.

2 Press and hold the left mouse button.

3 Move the mouse to drag the selected object.

In most cases, the object moves along with ⌖.

4 Release the mouse button when the selected object is repositioned where you want it.

Why does Windows 7 sometimes not recognize my double-clicks?
Try slowing the double-click speed using these steps. Click the **Start** button (⊞). Click **Devices and Printers** to display the Devices and Printers window. Right-click your mouse and click **Mouse settings** to display the Mouse Properties dialog box. In the Double-Click Speed group, click and drag the slider to the left, toward the Slow setting (●). You can also set up your mouse for a left-handed person by clicking (●) **Switch primary and secondary buttons** (☐ changes to ☑). Click **OK** to put the new settings into effect.

53

Explore Mouse Types

Two-Button Mouse

The standard mouse has a simple design with only two mouse buttons, although three-button mice where you can program the middle button are also available. You slide the mouse on your desktop to move the mouse pointer on-screen. The underside of an older mouse contains a small ball that rotates when you move the mouse. The newer style of optical mouse uses an optical sensor instead of a ball.

Wheel Mouse

A wheel mouse has a wheel that you can rotate, usually between the two buttons. In many programs, when you rotate the wheel forward, the document scrolls up, and when you rotate the wheel backward, the document scrolls down. The wheel is particularly useful when reviewing Web pages on the Internet.

Trackball

A trackball mouse is one in which the ball is visible instead of sitting underneath the mouse. When you use a trackball, you do not move the mouse; instead, you use your fingers or palm to rotate the ball. The rotational movement of the trackball moves the mouse pointer on-screen. Trackball mice are particularly useful in small spaces because the space allotted to the mouse is fixed.

Touch Pad

A touch pad is a flat, pressure-sensitive surface that is often used on netbooks or notebooks as the mouse input device. You can move the mouse pointer on-screen by moving your finger along the surface of the touch pad. You click by tapping the surface with your finger, although most touch pads also include left and right buttons for clicking.

Pointing Stick

Resembling a pencil eraser, a pointing stick is a rubber cylinder found on notebook computers. You control the directional movement of the mouse pointer on-screen by nudging the pointing stick in the direction you want to move the mouse pointer.

Digital Pen/Stylus

On a tablet PC, you can use the digital pen as a mouse. Hover the pen over the screen surface until you see the pointer, and then move the pen to move the pointer. Tap the screen surface to click.

Mouse Tips

Mouse Safety

Studies have shown that using the mouse excessively causes more repetitive stress injuries than excessively using the keyboard. To prevent overuse injuries related to mouse use, keep your mouse at the same height as your keyboard, use a mouse wrist rest, do not lean any portion of the arm you use for your mouse on the edge of the desktop to avoid cutting off blood flow circulation. You can also learn program shortcut keys to reduce your mouse use.

Do Not Forget to Right-Click

Most users master the left-click immediately, but they forget that they also can right-click. Right-clicking displays a shortcut menu relevant to the screen you are viewing or the action you are taking; if you learn to remember to right-click, you will save time and effort. If the choice you want does not appear on the shortcut menu, left-click outside the menu to close it.

Use an Optical Drive

You can use your computer's optical drive to insert a CD or DVD disc and access the files on the disc. If you have a recordable drive, you can burn your own files to a disc.

Most optical drives reside inside the computer case, but you can also add an external drive to your computer. This approach works well if you are using a netbook computer because it does not come with an optical drive; eliminating the optical drive is one way for computer vendors to reduce the size and weight of the computer.

Use an Optical Drive

Insert a CD or DVD Disc

1 Press the button in the front of the drive.

● The disc tray slides out.

2 Remove the disk from its case or sleeve.

Note: When you handle the disc, be sure to touch only its edges.

3 Place the disc, writing side up, in the drive's disc tray.

Note: The shiny surface faces down.

4 Press the drive button.

The disc tray closes.

Note: In many cases, inserting a disc causes the operating system to automatically either display the contents of the disc or start the program contained on the disc. Therefore, you may not need to run through the steps on the next page.

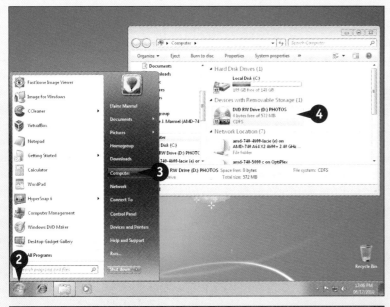

Display CD or DVD Contents

1. Insert the CD or DVD in the optical drive.

   If the AutoPlay window appears, click ⊠.

2. Click the **Start** button (🔘).

3. Click **Computer**.

   The Computer window appears.

4. Double-click the optical drive icon.

   Note: The name that appears beside the optical drive icon usually depends on the name given to the disc in the drive.

   The contents of the disc appear.

5. When you are done with the CD or DVD, click ⊠ to close the window.

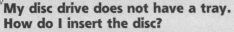

My disc drive does not have a tray. How do I insert the disc?	Why do I see a menu when I insert some discs?
Some optical drives have a narrow slot in the front of the drive. Insert your disc into that slot until it catches and inserts itself the rest of the way. Press the drive button to eject the disc.	Windows 7 recognizes certain types of discs, such as music CDs, when you insert them. Click the option that you prefer, and then click **OK**.

Use a USB Storage Device

You can use your computer's USB drives to connect and read external storage devices. External storage devices come in many types; you can connect an external hard drive that is rectangular in shape or a USB flash drive about the size and shape of your thumb. If your system does not come with a memory card reader, you can purchase an external one and attach it using a USB port.

When you have finished working with a USB storage device or memory card, you need to remove it correctly to avoid errors.

Use a USB Storage Device

Display the Contents of a USB Storage Device

① Connect the USB storage device into any USB port on your computer.

The AutoPlay window appears.

② Click **Open folder to view files using Windows Explorer**.

The contents of the USB storage device appear.

● The drive letter associated with the USB storage device appears here. In this example, the drive letter is F.

③ When you are done with the USB storage device, click ✕.

The window closes.

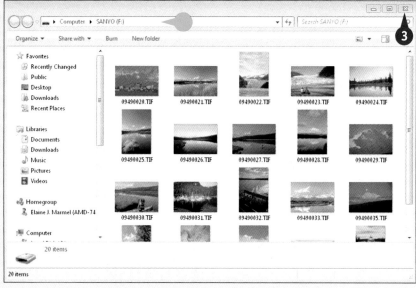

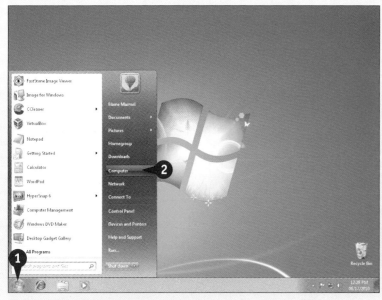

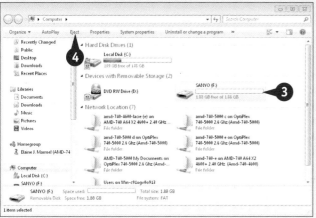

Remove a USB Storage Device

① Click the **Start** button ().

② Click **Computer**.

The Computer window appears.

③ Click the device icon that represents the USB storage device.

④ Click **Eject**.

If the USB storage device contents are currently open in a window, that window closes.

⑤ Remove the USB storage device from the USB port on your computer.

Simplify It

How do I insert a memory card?
Hold the card so that the label is facing up. Find the edge of the card that contains a series of small holes or metal contacts. Insert that edge into the memory card reader slot that is just wide enough to hold the card.

Does it matter which USB port I select to plug in my USB storage device?
No. On older computers, some USB ports operated at slower speeds than others. The USB ports on newer computers all operate at the fastest USB speed available — USB 2.0.

Restart the Computer

You can restart your computer, so that it shuts down and starts up again immediately. This is useful if your computer is running slowly or behaving oddly. Sometimes a restart solves the problem.

Some programs or devices you install require that you restart the system before they function properly. In addition, some updates to Windows require that you restart your computer to make them fully functional. Knowing how to restart your computer is useful under these circumstances because, if you are busy, then you can always decide to restart your computer at a more convenient time.

Restart the Computer

① Shut down all of your running programs.

Note: Be sure to save your work as you close your programs.

② Click the **Start** button (⊞).

③ Click the **Shut down** arrow (▷).

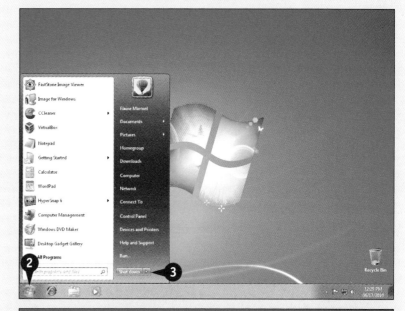

● A menu of options appears.

④ Click **Restart**.

Your computer shuts down and then restarts.

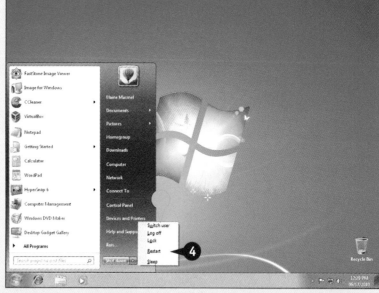

Turn Off the Computer

When you complete your work for the day, you should shut down your computer. Although some people leave their systems on all the time, you really do not need to waste electricity powering a device you are not using.

You should not simply shut off the computer's power; instead, follow the proper steps so that you avoid damaging files on your system.

Shutting off the computer's power without properly exiting programs and the operating system can cause two problems. First, if you have unsaved changes in some open documents, you lose those changes. Second, you could damage one or more operating system files, which could make your computer unstable.

Turn Off the Computer

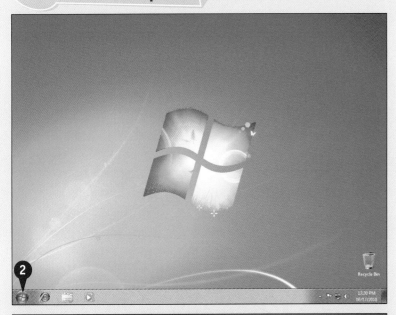

1 Shut down all of your running programs.

Note: *Be sure to save your work as you close your programs.*

2 Click the **Start** button (⊞).

● The Windows Start menu appears.

3 Click **Shut down**.

The operating system shuts down and your computer turns off.

Chapter 4

Learning Windows 7 Basics

Almost all new PCs have the Windows 7 operating system installed. You can use Windows 7 to start programs, manage files, connect to the Internet, and perform computer maintenance, and so having a basic understanding of how Windows 7 works is important. In this chapter, you learn about the Windows 7 screen and Start menu and how to work with programs.

Explore the Windows 7 Screen

Take a moment to become familiar with the basic screen elements of the Windows 7 operating system.

The entire screen is referred to as the *Windows desktop*, and you can store shortcuts to programs or Windows features on the desktop that you double-click to launch the program or feature. If you prefer, you can attach those shortcuts to the taskbar, which runs along the bottom of the desktop, or the Windows Start menu, which appears when you click the Start button, and simply click the shortcut to launch the program or feature. Read more about the Windows Start menu in the next section.

Mouse Pointer

When you move your mouse, this pointer moves along with it, identifying the location of the mouse pointer.

Desktop Shortcuts

A desktop icon represents a shortcut to a program or Windows 7 feature on your computer that you can double-click to start or launch.

Desktop

This is the Windows 7 work area, where you work with your programs and documents.

Show Desktop Button

Click this button to redisplay the Windows desktop if you have several programs open at once, and you need to see the desktop.

Date and Time

This is the current date and time on your computer based on the time zone you select when you install Windows.

Speaker Volume Indicator

Position the mouse pointer over this indicator to see the current speaker volume level; click the indicator to adjust the volume.

Internet Access Indicator

Position the mouse pointer over this button to see if you are currently connected to the Internet.

Actions Center

This area displays balloons that notify you about things happening on your computer.

Hidden Icons

Click this button to see programs running in the background, such as your antivirus program.

Start Button

Use this button to start programs and launch many of the Windows 7 features.

Taskbar

Buttons for programs that you have opened appear highlighted in the taskbar. Use this area to switch between programs.

Programs Pinned to the Taskbar

Pin programs you use frequently to the taskbar by right-clicking the program shortcut and choosing **Pin to Taskbar**. Click any button pinned to the taskbar to start that program.

Understanding the Start Menu

The Windows Start menu appears when you click the Start button and provides access to programs installed on your computer and Windows features such as the Windows Control Panel or the Devices and Printers window.

You can think of the Windows Start menu in two columns: The left column lists shortcuts to frequently used programs and the right column lists shortcuts to frequently used Windows features. The left column changes based on the programs you use, whereas the right column remains static. You can customize the left column to always display programs of your choice at the top.

Programs Pinned to the Start Menu

By default, no programs appear here, but you can add them by right-clicking a shortcut on your desktop or in a folder in the All Programs list and selecting **Pin to Start Menu**. Windows 7 then places a shortcut for that program permanently at the top of the Start menu; a line separates shortcuts pinned to the Start menu from shortcuts for frequently used programs.

Frequently Used Programs

This list initially displays common accessory programs included with Windows 7. You can customize the list to instead display programs you open frequently based on your usage.

User Account Picture

This small picture is associated with the account you use to log into Windows. You can change this picture.

Windows Features

Commonly used Windows features appear here; you can customize this list to include or exclude features.

Start Button

Use this button to open and display the Windows Start menu.

Search Bar

You can search for files, programs, and help by clicking in the Search bar and typing something that represents what you want to find.

All Programs

Click here to see a list of the programs installed on your computer. Most appear in folders, and you can start the programs using the items listed in the folder; see the next section for details.

Start a Program

To work with any program, you must first tell Windows 7 what program you want to run. To launch a program, you can use the Windows Start menu. The All Programs command on the Start menu displays a list of folders representing the programs installed on your computer; each folder contains shortcuts that launch programs.

You also can launch a program by double-clicking a desktop shortcut if your program installed one, selecting an item that appears in the Frequently Used Program list on the Start menu, or clicking an item pinned to the Start menu or the Windows taskbar.

Start a Program

1 Click the **Start** button (🏁).

The Start menu appears.

Note: *If the program you want to launch appears on the Start menu, click the program and skip the rest of the steps in this section.*

2 Click **All Programs**.

The All Programs menu appears.

Note: *When you click All Programs, the All Programs command changes to Back.*

3 Click the folder that contains your program.

Note: *Shortcuts that launch programs can appear directly on the All Programs menu or in folders.*

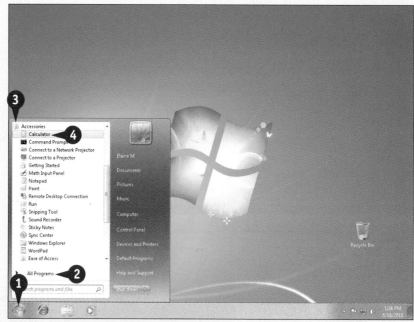

4 Click the shortcut for the program that you want to start.

● The program appears on the desktop.

● Windows 7 adds a highlighted button for the program to the taskbar.

Note: *To shut down a program when you finish using it, press* Alt + F4 *or click the* **Close** *button (🗙).*

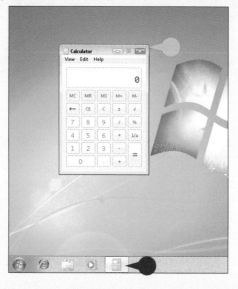

Tour a Program Window

When you start a program, it appears on the Windows 7 desktop in its own window; either the program's window fills the screen, hiding the desktop, or you can see the desktop behind the program's window. Using options in the program's window, you can control whether the program fills the screen or displays the Windows desktop in the background.

You work with a program using the various features in its window, and all Windows programs share most of the features described in this section.

System Menu Button

Click this button to move, size, and perform other program window actions using the keyboard.

Toolbar

The toolbar contains buttons that offer easy access to common program commands and features without opening menus or changing Ribbon tabs. In programs that contain a Ribbon, the toolbar is called the Quick Access Toolbar.

Title Bar

The title bar displays the name of the program and, in some programs, the name of the open document. To move the window, click and drag the title bar.

Minimize Button

Click the **Minimize** button (⬜) to hide the window and display only a button in the Windows taskbar that represents the window.

Maximize Button

Click the **Maximize** button (⬜) to enlarge the window so that it fills the entire screen and hides the Windows desktop. The Maximize button then changes to the Restore button; click the **Restore** button (⬜) to display the window with a portion of the Windows desktop visible in the background.

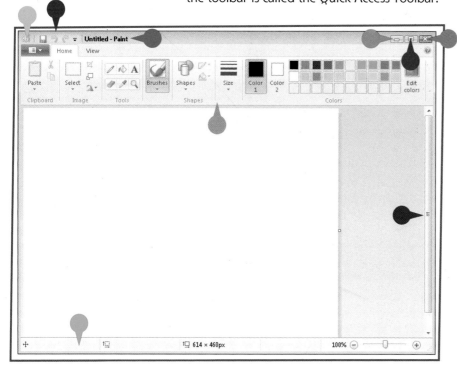

Close Button

When you click the **Close** button (❌), the program shuts down.

Ribbon

Many newer programs use a Ribbon that replaces the menu bar. These programs usually still contain a toolbar, but it appears above the Ribbon and beside the system menu button.

Status Bar

The status bar displays information about the current state of the program or document.

Scrollbar

Use the scroll bar to navigate a document. In a vertical scroll bar, click **Scroll Up** (▲) to navigate up, and click **Scroll Down** (▼) to navigate down. You can use a horizontal scroll bar to navigate left and right in a document.

Select a Command Using the Ribbon

The Ribbon contains the commands you use to operate the program. The Ribbon is organized in three components: tabs, groups, and commands. Tabs represent common actions you take in the program. They appear across the top of the Ribbon. In some programs, such as Microsoft Word or Excel, you find context-sensitive tabs that appear only when you need them.

On each Ribbon tab, you find buttons representing commands. The buttons are organized into groups of related commands, and the name of each group appears below that group on the Ribbon. You can choose a command from the Ribbon using either the keyboard or the mouse.

Select a Command Using the Ribbon

Use the Keyboard

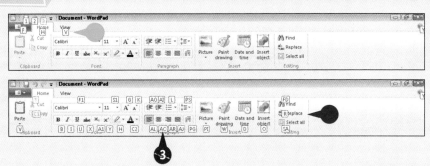

1 Press Alt.

● Shortcut letters and numbers appear on the Ribbon and the Quick Access Toolbar.

2 Press a letter to select a tab on the Ribbon.

This example uses H to select the Home tab.

● The appropriate tab appears, displaying letters for each command on that tab.

3 Press a letter or letters to select a command.

● Options for the command you selected appear if necessary; otherwise, the program performs the command.

Use the Mouse

❶ Click the tab containing the command.

❷ Click the command.

● The program performs the command.

What is the Quick Access Toolbar?
Early versions of Microsoft programs contained menus and multiple toolbars. Later versions of Microsoft programs contain the Ribbon and only one toolbar, the Quick Access Toolbar, and the Quick Access Toolbar contains the most commonly used commands, such as Save or Undo. If you click 🔽, you can add commands to the Quick Access Toolbar to customize it.

What should I do if I press the wrong letter for a tab?
You can press Esc. The program again displays the letters and numbers for the tabs and Quick Access Toolbar.

Select a Command Using a Menu or Toolbar

Many programs have a combination of menus and toolbars you can use to perform various functions in the program. Menus display a list of commands you can select, like a restaurant's menu presents the choices of food you can order. Computer program menus are also called *drop-down menus* because the list of commands "drops down" on-screen when you open the menu.

Many programs display one or more toolbars, usually at the top of the application window below the menus. Toolbars are collections of buttons representing commands on menus; toolbars enable you to access the program's most common features quickly with a single click.

Select a Command Using a Menu or Toolbar

Select a Menu Command

1 Click the name of the menu that you want to display.

● The program displays the menu.

2 Click the command that you want to run.

The program performs the command.

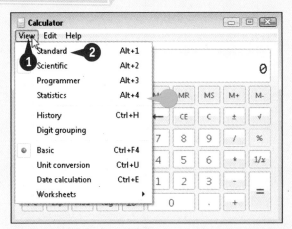

Select a Toolbar Command

1 Click the toolbar button that represents the command.

● The program runs the command.

Note: If the toolbar button appears "pressed" after you click it, the button toggles a feature on or off, and that feature is now on. To turn the feature off, click the button again.

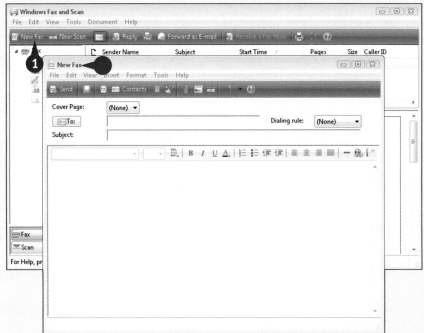

Understanding Dialog Box Options

You use dialog boxes to provide information to a program. For example, a dialog box in a word-processing application like Microsoft Word or Corel WordPerfect contains controls that enable you to select page margins. You provide information using the various types of options in the dialog box.

Dialog boxes appear when you click any command on a menu that has ellipses (...) after its name or when you click a dialog box launcher button in the lower right corner of a group on a Ribbon. None of the programs included in Windows 7 have dialog box launcher buttons, but programs you buy, such as Microsoft Word or Excel, contain them.

Tab

Dialog boxes contain tabs to help organize all of the available choices. If necessary, a dialog box can contain multiple tabs.

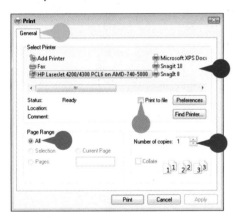

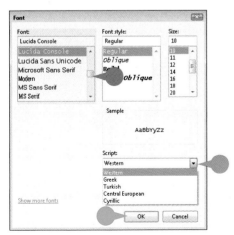

List Box

A list box displays a relatively large number of choices in either a horizontal or vertical list. If you do not see the item you want to select, you can click the scroll arrows on either end of the list box's scroll bar.

Option Button

You can click one option button in any group of option buttons to make a selection. When you click an option button, it changes from ◎ to ◉.

Combo Box

The combo box combines both a text box and a list box. The list box displays a list of choices from which you select the item you want. To select an item, you can click an item in the list or type a list item's name in the text box.

Command Button

You can click a command button to run the command written on the button face. For example, you can click **OK** to apply settings that you choose in a dialog box, or you can click **Cancel** to close the dialog box without changing the settings.

Check Box

You can click a check box to make a selection and click the check box again to cancel the selection. If you click a check box to make a selection, the check box changes from ☐ to ☑. When you cancel a selection, the check box changes from ☑ to ☐.

Spin Button

The spin button (⬍) enables you to choose a numeric value using your mouse. You also can type the value in the text box beside the spin button.

Drop-Down List Box

A drop-down list box displays only the selected item from a list. You can click the arrow (▾) beside the list to select a different item.

Use Dialog Box Controls

You can use options in dialog boxes to control how a program behaves. Dialog boxes appear frequently, enabling you to specify settings for different features in the program. Suppose that you want to print a document. You can display the Print dialog box to control the way the document prints. For example, you can select a printer from those listed in the dialog box, use option buttons to specify how much of the document you want to print, and use spinner buttons to identify the number of copies that you want to print.

Use Dialog Box Controls

Type Text in a Text Box

1 Click inside the text box.

● A blinking, vertical bar called the insertion point appears inside the text box.

Note: *Some people mistakenly call the insertion point the cursor.*

2 Press `Backspace` or `Delete` to delete any existing characters.

3 Type your text.

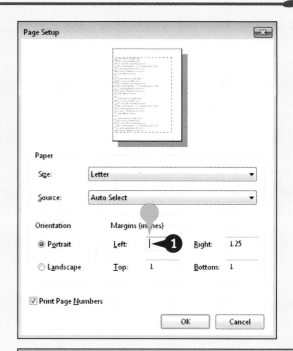

Enter a Value with a Spin Box

1 Click the top arrow in the spinner box (⊟) to increase the value.

2 Click the bottom arrow to decrease the value.

● You can also type the value in the text box.

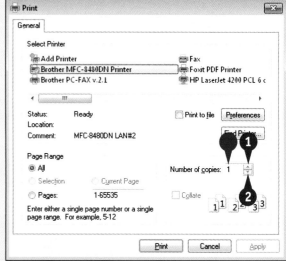

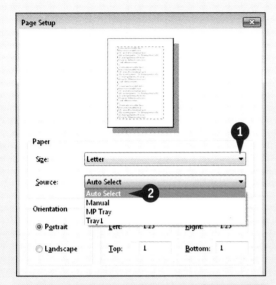

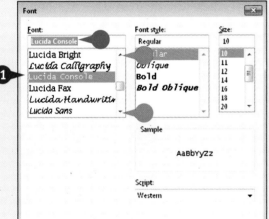

Select a Drop-Down List Box Item

1 Click ⊡ to open the list and display the item that you want to select.

2 Click the item.

The list box closes, and your selection appears.

Select an Item from a Combo Box

1 Click the item that you want to select.

● You can type the item name in the text box.

● If you cannot see the item you want to select, click ⊡ or ⊡ to scroll through the list and find it.

Are there keyboard shortcuts that I can use to make it easier to work with dialog boxes?
Yes. Here are the most useful shortcuts:

Enter	Selects the default command button, which is indicated with a highlight around it.
Esc	Closes the dialog box without making any changes. This action is the same as clicking Cancel.
Alt + letter	Selects the control that contains the underlined letter.
Tab	Moves forward through the dialog box controls.
Shift + **Tab**	Moves backward through the dialog box controls.
⬆ and ⬇	Moves up and down within the current option button group.
Alt + ⬇	Displays the selected combo box or drop-down list box.

Save a Document

You save a document to preserve the work you have done on the document. If you save your document, you also can close the program, shut down your computer, come back another day or time, and reopen the document to make changes to it.

While you work on a document, the program you are using stores the changes you make to the document in your computer's memory. When you close the program, it erases the information it stored in memory. If you save your document before you close the program, you preserve your changes on your computer's hard drive.

Save a Document

① Click the **File** button (▣).

Note: *Several Windows 7 programs use a Ribbon interface that does not display File.*

② Click **Save**.

● In most programs, you can also press Ctrl + S or click the **Save** button (▣).

If you have saved the document previously, your changes are now preserved, and you can skip the rest of the steps in this section.

If you have not previously saved this document, the Save As dialog box appears.

● Most programs automatically select the Documents folder as the storage location for the file.

● If you want to save the document elsewhere, click the name of the folder in this list.

● If you want to create a new folder, click **New folder**, type the folder name, and then press Enter.

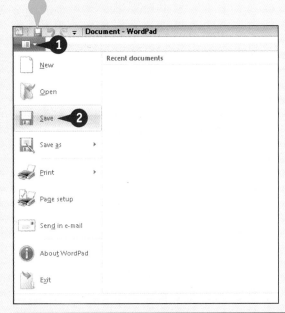

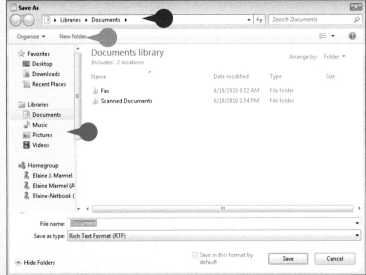

③ Click in the File name text box and type a name for the document.

Note: *The filename can be up to 255 characters long; it cannot include the following characters:* < > , ? : " | *.

④ Click **Save**.

● The filename that you typed appears in the program's title bar.

Simplify It

Can I create different types of documents in a program?
Yes, in some cases. Using WordPad you can create word-processing documents, which can contain both text and graphics, and text documents, which can contain only text. However, Notepad supports only text documents. If the program supports multiple document types, the Save As dialog box usually has a drop-down list called Save As Type. Use that list to choose the document type that you want.

Can anyone open and read my documents?
Anyone using any version of Windows can read documents you create in any program that ships with Windows.

Open a Document

To work with a document that you have saved in the past, you can open it in the program that you used to create it.

Typically, when you finish working on a document and save it, you exit from the program, closing the document; in the background, Windows 7 keeps a record of where, on your hard drive, the file resides. To make changes to the document, you open it. When you open a document, Windows 7 locates the file on your hard drive and passes the location information to the program so that the program can redisplay the document on-screen.

Open a Document

1 Start the program you want to use.

2 Click the **File** button (▣).

Note: If you see a list of the most recently opened documents and the document you want appears in the list, click the name to open it. You can then skip the rest of the steps.

3 Click **Open**.

In most programs, you can also press Ctrl + O.

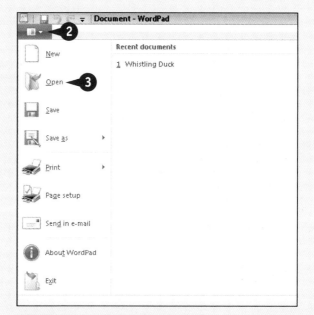

The Open dialog box appears.

● Most programs automatically display the contents of the Documents folder.

● If you want to display a different folder, click the name of the folder in this list.

● If you stored the document in a folder inside the Documents folder, double-click that folder here.

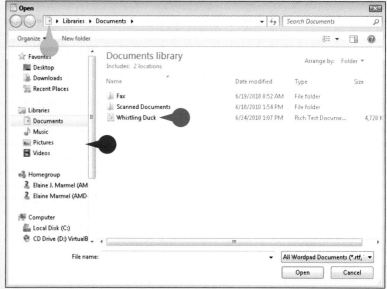

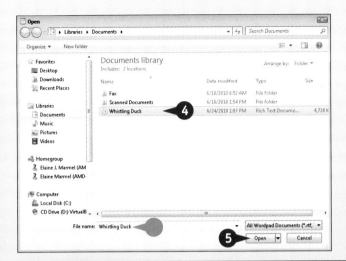

④ Click the document.

● The name of the document you select appears here.

⑤ Click **Open**.

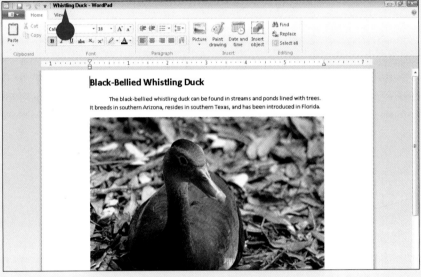

● The document appears in the program window.

Black-Bellied Whistling Duck

The black-bellied whistling duck can be found in streams and ponds lined with trees. It breeds in southern Arizona, resides in southern Texas, and has been introduced in Florida.

Simplify It

Is there another way to open a document?
Yes. You can open the folder that contains the document and then double-click the document. Windows 7 automatically launches the program and opens the document. To do so, click the **Start** button (🔘) and then click **Documents** to display the Documents folder. Double-click the document. Windows 7 starts the program in which you created the document and opens the document.

Switch Between Open Programs

In Windows 7, you can run more than one program simultaneously — a technique known as *multitasking*. For example, you can work on a word-processing document, use your e-mail program, and browse the Web. The number of programs you can use simultaneously is limited only by the amount of memory each program needs and the amount of memory in your computer.

When you multitask, you need to know how to switch from one program to another using either the mouse or the keyboard. If you are using one of the Aero themes in Windows 7, you also can use Aero Flip 3D to switch between open programs and windows.

Switch Between Open Programs

Switch Using the Taskbar

1 Open at least two different programs using the steps in the section "Start a Program."

● You can position the mouse pointer over a taskbar button to see the name of the program and open the document in that program.

2 Click the taskbar button of the program to which you want to switch.

● Windows 7 brings the program window to the foreground.

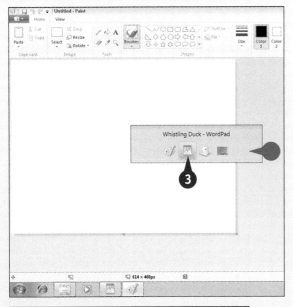

Switch Using the Keyboard

1 Open at least two different programs using the steps in the section "Start a Program."

2 Press **Alt** + **Tab**.

● Windows 7 displays thumbnail versions of the open windows.

3 Press **Tab** repeatedly until Windows 7 selects the program you want to use.

4 Release **Alt**.

● The program you selected appears in the foreground of your screen.

Simplify It

How do I use Aero Flip 3D?
Press and hold ⊞ and then press **Tab**. Windows 7 displays a 3D rendering of all open windows. Repeatedly pressing **Tab** brings the next window in the stack to the forefront. Aero Flip 3D displays the contents of the window rather than thumbnail representations. Release ⊞ when you find the window you want to use.

Print a Document

When you need a paper copy of your document, either for your files or to distribute to someone else, you can send the document to your printer. If you have more than one printer, you can specify the printer you want to use. Before you print, you can indicate the number of copies you want to print and, in many programs, you can opt to print only a part of your document; for example, you can print selected text, a particular page, or a range of pages.

Before printing, be sure to turn on your printer and check that it has enough paper.

Print a Document

① Open the document that you want to print.

② Click the **File** button (▤).

③ Click **Print**.

Note: In many programs, you can select the Print command by pressing Ctrl + P.

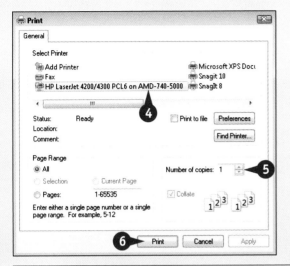

The Print dialog box appears.

Note: *The layout of the Print dialog box varies from program to program. The WordPad version shown here is a typical example.*

④ If you have more than one printer, click the printer that you want to use.

⑤ Click the **Number of copies** ⬍ to specify the number of copies that you want to print.

⑥ Click **Print**.

In many programs, you can send a document directly to the printer by clicking the **Print** button (🖶).

Windows 7 prints the document.

● The print icon appears in the taskbar's Notification area while the document prints.

Black-Bellied Whistling Duck

The black-bellied whistling duck can be found in streams and ponds lined with trees. It breeds in southern Arizona, resides in southern Texas, and has been introduced in Florida.

Simplify It

How do I print only part of a document?
● Print selected text: Select the text that you want to print. In the Print dialog box, click the **Selection** option (◎ changes to ◉).
● Print a specific page: Place the insertion point on the page that you want to print. In the Print dialog box, click the **Current Page** option (◎ changes to ◉).
● Print a range of pages: In the Print dialog box, click the **Pages** option (◎ changes to ◉) and type the first page number, then a dash (–), and then the last page number.

Edit Document Text

When you work with a character-based file, such as a text or word-processing document or an e-mail message, you need to know the basic techniques for editing text. The four fundamental editing actions you take are deleting, selecting, copying, and moving text.

Deleting text does exactly what you expect: It removes information from a document, and you can use the [Delete] and [Backspace] keys to delete characters.

You select text to identify the text you want to work on. You select text to delete it, underline it, align it, change its size, copy it, or move it.

Delete Characters

1 In a text document, click immediately to the left of the first character that you want to delete.

● The insertion point appears before the character.

2 Press [Delete] until you have deleted all the characters that you want removed.

● The characters disappear from the document.

Note: *An alternative method is to click immediately to the right of the last character that you want to delete and then to press* [Backspace] *until you have deleted all necessary characters.*

Note: *If you make a mistake, immediately click* **Edit**, *and then click* **Undo**. *You can also press* [Ctrl] + [Z] *or click the* **Undo** *button (⬚).*

Physical Characteristics

Generally, 20-22", the black-bellied whistling duck is a large, long-legged, long-necked duck. The adult has a bright orange bill, pink legs, a gray face and upper neck with white eye ring. This duck sports a chestnut cap, nape, lower neck, chest and back, and a black belly. White secondary coverts and white bases to the black primaries and secondaries create a long wing stripe in flight and a visible pale patch at rest.

Physical Characteristics

Generally, the black-bellied whistling duck is a large, long-legged, long-necked duck. The adult has a bright orange bill, pink legs, a gray face and upper neck with white eye ring. This duck sports a chestnut cap, nape, lower neck, chest and back, and a black belly. White secondary coverts and white bases to the black primaries and secondaries create a long wing stripe in flight and a visible pale patch at rest.

Physical Characteristics

Generally 20-22", the black-bellied whistling duck is a large, long-legged, long-necked duck. The adult has a bright orange bill, pink legs, a gray face and upper neck with white eye ring. This duck sports a chestnut cap, nape, lower neck, chest and back, and a black belly. White secondary coverts and white bases to the black primaries and secondaries create a long wing stripe in flight and a visible pale patch at rest.

Physical Characteristics

Generally 20-22", the black-bellied whistling duck is a large, long-legged, long-necked duck. The adult has a bright orange bill, pink legs, a gray face and upper neck with white eye ring. This duck sports a chestnut cap, nape, lower neck, chest and back, and a black belly. White secondary coverts and white bases to the black primaries and secondaries create a long wing stripe in flight and a visible pale patch at rest.

Select Text for Editing

1 Click immediately to the left of the first character you want to select.

2 Click and drag across the text that you want to select.

3 Release the mouse button.

● The program highlights the selected text.

Simplify It

Are there any shortcut methods for selecting text in WordPad?
Yes. Here are the most useful ones:

● Click in the white space to the left of a line to select the line.

● Double-click a word to select it.

● Triple-click inside a paragraph to select it.

● Press `Ctrl` + `A` to select the entire document.

continued

Edit Document Text *(continued)*

Once you select text, you can then copy or move the text to another location in your document.

You move text to change its location in a document. For example, after typing information, you might decide that it would make more sense in a different place in the document.

You copy text when you want to repeat the exact same information in another location. Copying information from one place in a document to another and then changing information can be faster than retyping the information. For example, if a list of items is similar, copy the first and then edit the subsequent occurrences.

Edit Document Text *(continued)*

Move Text

1 Select the text that you want to move.

2 Click the **Cut** button (🔲).

Note: *In most programs, you can also press* Ctrl + X.

Note: *In programs without a Ribbon, click the* **Edit** *menu and then click* **Cut**.

The program removes the text from the document.

3 Click in the document at the position where you want to move the text.

4 Click the **Paste** button (🔲).

Note: *In most programs, you can also press* Ctrl + V.

Note: *In programs without a Ribbon, click the* **Edit** *menu and then click* **Paste**.

● The program inserts the text at the position of the insertion point.

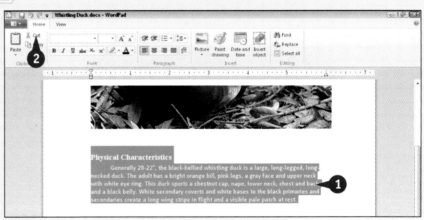

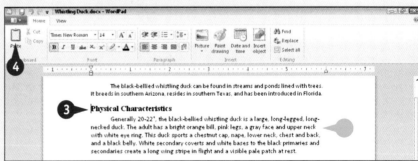

Copy Text

1 Select the text that you want to copy.

2 Click the **Copy** button ().

Note: In most programs, you can also press Ctrl + C.

*Note: In programs without a Ribbon, click the **Edit** menu and then click **Copy**.*

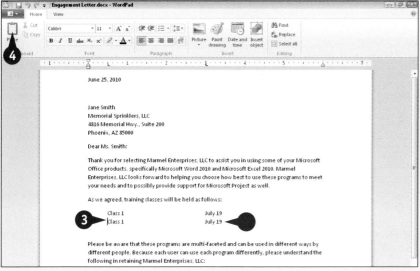

3 Click in the document at the position where you want the copy of the text to appear.

4 Click the **Paste** button (⬚).

Note: In most programs, you can also press Ctrl + V.

*Note: In programs without a Ribbon, click the **Edit** menu and then click **Paste**.*

● The program inserts a copy of the selected text at the position of the insertion point.

Simplify It

Can I move and copy text using only my mouse?
Yes, you can. Select the text that you want to move or copy as described in the section "Select Text for Editing." To move the selected text, position ▷ over the selection and click and drag the text to the new position within the document. As you drag, the mouse pointer changes to ▷.

To copy the selected text, position ▷ over the selection, press and hold Ctrl, and click and drag the text to the new position within the document. As you drag, the mouse pointer changes to ▷.

Start Frequently Used Programs

You can set up Windows 7 so that you can easily find and start frequently used programs with the Windows 7 *pin* feature. *Pinning* is the process of attaching a program to the Windows Start menu or the Windows taskbar, or both.

All of the programs installed on your computer appear on the Windows 7 All Programs menu,

and most place an icon on the desktop that you can double-click to open. But, pinning the programs you use very regularly — like your e-mail program or your browser — to the top of the Start menu or the Windows taskbar makes these programs readily accessible.

Start Frequently Used Programs

1 Click the **Start** button (🔘).

2 Click **All Programs**.

3 Click the folder containing the program you want to pin to the Start menu or the taskbar.

● Windows opens the folder and displays its contents.

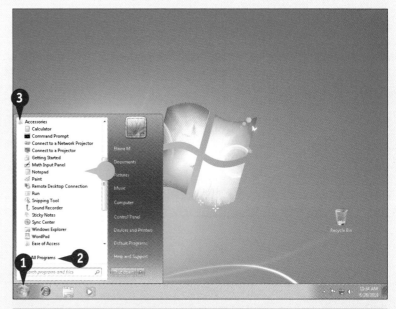

4 Right-click the button you use to start the program.

5 Click **Pin to Start Menu** or **Pin to Taskbar**, depending on where you want the program's icon to appear.

Note: *This example demonstrates pinning a program to the Start menu.*

6 Click **Back**.

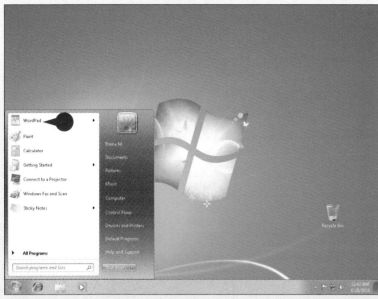

● The program appears at the top of the Start menu.

Note: *Each time you click the **Start** button ( ), the program appears at the top of the Start menu, and you can start the program by clicking the entry at the top of the Start menu.*

● If you clicked **Pin to Taskbar** in Step **5**, Windows places a button for the program on the Windows taskbar.

You can start the program by clicking its button on the Windows taskbar.

Simplify It

Why should I pin programs to the Start menu or taskbar instead of using a desktop icon to start a program?
Pinning programs gives you, at your fingertips, the programs you use most often, and you can eliminate desktop icons to make your desktop neater. You can leave icons for programs you use rarely in their All Programs folders and pin icons for programs you use regularly.

Can I pin programs to the bottom of the Start menu?
No, but if you customize the Start menu, programs you use frequently will appear at the bottom of the Start menu.

Customize the Start Menu

You can customize the Windows Start menu so that it looks and functions in a way that best supports how you work. For example, you can turn off the highlighting that Windows automatically applies to new programs you install.

On the left side of the Start menu, you can have Windows display a list of programs you have recently opened, and you can control the number of programs Windows lists.

You also can control some of the entries that appear on the right side of the Start menu, adding items you feel you need and removing items you feel you do not need.

Customize the Start Menu

1 Right-click any empty space on the Windows taskbar.

2 From the shortcut menu that appears, click **Properties**.

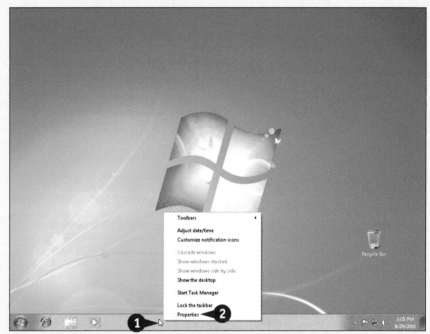

The Taskbar and Start Menu Properties dialog box appears.

3 Click the **Start Menu** tab.

4 If you do not want Windows 7 to list your recently used programs, click here (☑ changes to ☐).

5 If you do not want Windows 7 to list recently used documents beside programs on the Start menu, click here (☑ changes to ☐).

6 Click **Customize**.

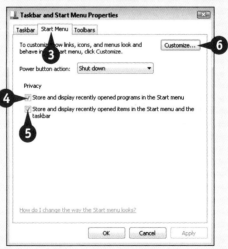

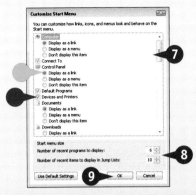

The Customize Start Menu dialog box appears.

7 Use the items in the list box to control what appears on the right side of the Start menu.

● Some items display options buttons; click the option you want (◎ changes to ◉).

● Some items display check boxes that determine whether the item appears (☑) or does not appear (☐) on the right side of the Start menu.

8 Click 🗘 to control the maximum number of recent programs displayed on the Start menu and recent items displayed in Jump lists.

9 Click **OK** twice to save your choices.

● The Windows Start menu reflects your choices.

Simplify It

How do I make Windows 7 stop highlighting new programs I install?

1 Follow Steps **1** to **7** in this section.

2 In the Customize Start Menu dialog box, scroll down in the list.

3 Click **Highlight newly installed programs** (☑ changes to ☐).

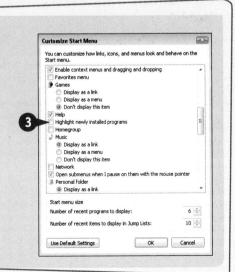

Customize
the Taskbar

You can customize the way the Windows taskbar looks and functions to make it suit the way you work. For example, you can change the size of the taskbar, making it taller. You might like this arrangement if you open lots of programs at the same time, because the program icons appear less crowded on a taller

taskbar. Or, you can opt to use smaller icons to represent open programs; this approach also enables you to display lots of program icons without changing the size of the taskbar.

You might want to temporarily hide the taskbar to display more of the programs you have open.

Customize the Taskbar

① Right-click any empty space on the Windows taskbar.

② From the shortcut menu that appears, click **Properties**.

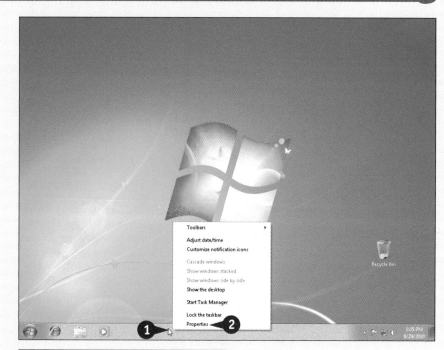

The Taskbar and Start Menu Properties dialog box appears.

③ Click **Lock the taskbar** (☑ changes to ☐).

Note: *By unlocking the taskbar, you can resize it.*

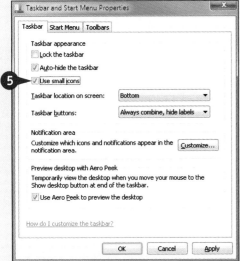

④ Click **Auto-hide the taskbar**
(☐ changes to ☑) to
temporarily hide the taskbar
while you work.

Note: *To display the hidden
taskbar, slide the mouse pointer
to the bottom edge of the screen
where the taskbar usually would
appear.*

⑤ Click **Use small icons**
(☐ changes to ☑) so that
you can fit more icons on
the taskbar.

How do I resize the taskbar to make it taller?
Follow Steps **1** to **3** in this section to unlock the taskbar.
Then, click and drag the top edge of the taskbar up. You
can add multiple rows to the taskbar and simultaneously
reduce the space allotted to an open program. To reduce
the taskbar's size, click and drag the top edge of the
taskbar down.

**What does the Aero Peek
option do?**
When enabled, you can temporarily
display your desktop by positioning
the mouse pointer over the vertical
bar at the right edge of the taskbar,
without clicking.

Customize the Taskbar *(continued)*

You also can change the location of the taskbar; it does not need to appear at the bottom of the screen. If you want, you can place it at the top of the screen or on either side of the screen.

You also can choose whether you want to group all windows from a given program on one taskbar button or display separate taskbar buttons for each open window.

The Notifications area appears by default at the right edge of the taskbar; you can determine which programs display icons in the Notifications area, and you can choose which system icons — like the date and time — appear in the system tray.

Customize the Taskbar *(continued)*

6 Click the **Taskbar location on screen** ⊡ and click a location for the taskbar.

7 Click the **Taskbar buttons** ⊡.

8 Click a grouping option for taskbar buttons.

Note: *See the tip on the next page to read about your choices.*

9 Click **Customize**.

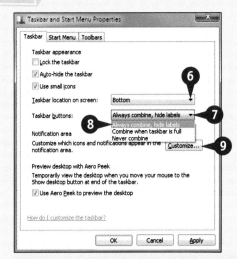

The Notification Area Icons window appears.

10 For each icon in the Notification area, click ⊡ and select the setting you prefer.

Note: *See the tip below to read about your choices.*

● You can display any notifications you have hidden if you click here.

11 Click **Turn system icons on or off**.

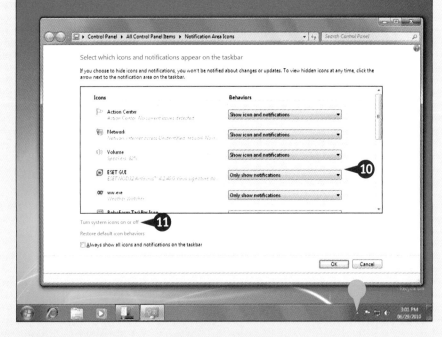

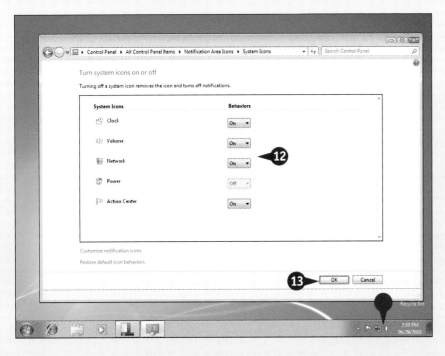

⓬ Click ▼ in the Behaviors column beside any system icon and click **On** or **Off**.

● Each system icon for which you click **On** appears in the system tray.

⓭ Click **OK** three times to save your choices.

What do the choices in the Taskbar Buttons list box mean?
You can group taskbar buttons to display only a single button for a program in which you have opened multiple windows. To switch between the open windows, click the program's button and then click the name of the window you want to view.

What do the options for the Notifications Area icons mean?
You use these options to control whether a Windows 7 displays a program's icon in the Notifications Area and messages from the program.

Select a Desktop Theme and Screen Saver

You can opt to use a desktop theme to spruce up the appearance of the Windows 7 desktop. The theme you select changes the desktop background and affects the color of the Windows taskbar and the title bars of all dialog boxes.

You also can select a screen saver — a moving pattern that Windows 7 displays after your

computer has been idle for a time period. The screen saver provides an interesting pattern on-screen and hides any work you might have been doing when you walked away from the computer. You also can have Windows 7 prompt you for your logon password when you return to your computer.

Select a Desktop Theme and Screen Saver

Set a Background

1. Right-click any blank space on the Windows desktop.

2. From the shortcut menu that appears, click **Personalize**.

The Personalization window appears.

3. Click a theme.

Note: *Use the scroll bar on the right side of the window to see more themes.*

● Windows 7 applies the theme to your desktop.

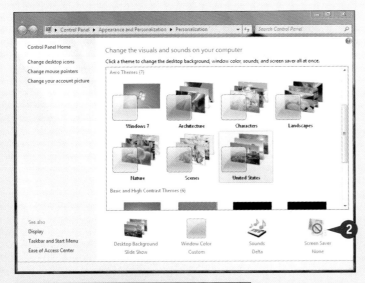

Select a Screen Saver

① Complete Steps **1** and **2** in the preceding section.

② Click **Screen Saver**.

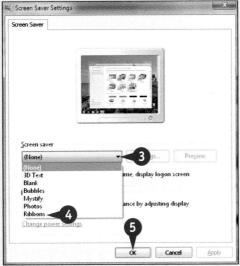

The Screen Saver Settings dialog box appears.

③ Click ⊟ to display a list of available screen savers.

④ Click a screen saver.

⑤ Click **OK**.

Simplify It

How do I set the amount of time to wait before the screen saver appears and control whether Windows 7 prompts for my password when I return to my computer?

In the Screen Saver Settings dialog box, use the **Wait** ⊟ to set the number of minutes. Click the **On resume, display logon screen** check box (☐ changes to ☑) to have Windows prompt you for your password before it permits use of the computer.

Chapter 5

Managing Files and Folders

Your computer stores all of the information you create in files. You can place these files in folders just the way you would place papers in folders that you store in a file cabinet. And, just as you manage the information in your file cabinet, you can manage the files and folders on your computer using the techniques described in this chapter.

Understanding How Windows Organizes Data

Every time you save something on your computer, you create a file. You open that file to make changes to the information in it, so you need to know where you put it when you saved it. You can think of a file in the same way you think of a paper document: it contains information.

Windows 7, the operating system, helps you organize information by enabling you to create folders in which to place your files. You can think of folders on your computer the same way you think of file folders that you place in a file cabinet.

Files

Everything you save on your computer is saved as a *file*. A file is nothing more than an electronic version of paper documents that contain information. A file can contain multiple pages of information, so, there is no one-to-one correspondence between paper and its electronic counterpart. A file can be as big or as small as it needs to be.

Folders

You can use folders to organize files, the same way you use file folders to organize paper documents. On your computer, when you save a file, you can place it in a folder. You can have as many folders as you want on your computer.

Libraries

Windows 7 automatically creates four *libraries* where you can store files of a similar type. Already set up on your computer, you will find the Documents, Music, Pictures, and Videos libraries, and each library contains two folders: a "My" version and a "Public" version of the library name. You can use libraries to share information across computers.

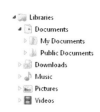

Create Folders

You are not limited to the folders in the libraries that Windows 7 creates; you can create your own folders. For example, you can create a folder called "My homework" in which you keep your homework assignments.

Place Folders within Folders

To help you organize, you can place folders, often called *subfolders*, inside other folders. In the Documents folder, you might create a folder called Tax Documents and store in it e-mailed receipts for charitable contributions and tax-related information. In the Pictures folder, you can create folders for each year and, inside those folders, you can create folders related to trips or events, almost like color-coding folders.

Reorganize Information

You can reorganize files by copying, moving, or renaming them. Suppose that you create a folder for all e-mail attachments and then receive one that also belongs in your Tax Documents folder. When you are not sure where to store a document, you can make a copy and store it in both places. See "Copy a File," "Move a File," and "Rename a File" later in this chapter.

Cleaning House

After you use your computer for a while, you will find you no longer need some files; you can delete them. When the Windows Recycle Bin contains deleted files, it appears full; to truly clean house, you "take out the trash." See "Delete a File" later in this chapter.

View Files

Once you create a file, you can view it, along with other files that might have been created by programs upon installation. You use Windows Explorer, a program that comes with Windows, to view files on your computer.

Most people store the files they work with in one of the main libraries associated with their user account: Documents, Music, Pictures, and Videos. In this section, you meet Windows Explorer, the program you use to browse for and work with your files. Using Windows Explorer, you can find and open folders and *subfolders* — folders inside folders.

View Files

1 Click the Windows Explorer button on the Windows taskbar.

Windows Explorer appears.

● The Navigation pane displays the main folders on your computer.

● The Details pane displays the contents of any folder you click in the Navigation pane.

Arrows beside folders in the Navigation pane indicate whether a folder is open or closed.

● A downward-pointing arrow (▣) indicates that the folder is open.

● A right-pointing arrow (▷) indicates a folder is closed.

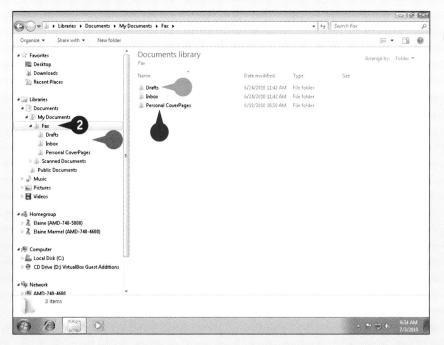

2 Double-click any folder in the Navigation pane.

● Windows Explorer displays the contents of the folder in the Details pane.

● Subfolders also appear on the Navigation pane, indented under the folder you double-clicked in Step **2**.

Note: Clicking any right-pointing arrow beside a folder has the same effect as double-clicking the folder.

● You can double-click a folder in the Details pane to open it.

Note: If you double-click a file instead of a folder, the program that created the file opens and displays the file.

Simplify It

Can I preview the contents of files?
Yes. You can click here (●) to hide or display the Preview pane; when displayed, it appears to the right of the Details pane. You click any file and its content appears in the Preview pane.

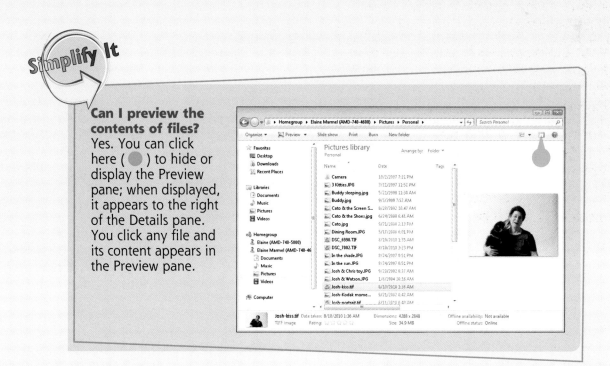

Become Familiar with the Windows Explorer Screen

You use Windows Explorer, a program that comes with Windows, for most of your work with files. The Windows Explorer screen is divided into two panes: the Navigation pane on the left side and the Details pane on the right. When you click an item in the Navigation pane, its contents appear in the Details pane.

The elements in the Navigation pane represent locations for folders on your computer and in your network. You can double-click any element in the Navigation pane to view its folders.

The Address bar displays the currently selected folder. The Search box helps you find files and folders. A context-sensitive toolbar helps you work with files and folders.

Favorites

Favorites are folders you use all the time and appear at the top of the Windows Explorer Navigation pane. Windows 7 sets up three favorites for you: Desktop, Downloads, and Recent Places. To add a folder to favorites, click the folder you want to add and then right-click **Favorites**. From the shortcut menu that appears, click **Add current location to favorites**.

Libraries

Libraries are very similar to folders, but they can be more than folders. Folders contain files, and although libraries contain files, they also can contain links to files and folders anywhere on your computer or any computer on the network. Windows 7 creates four libraries for each user account: Documents, Music, Pictures, and Videos.

Homegroup

The Homegroup entry in Windows Explorer identifies computers on a network. The computers in the Homegroup can each be set up to share the Documents, Music, Pictures, and Videos libraries as well as printers connected to any computer on the network.

Computer

The Computer entry in Windows Explorer shows the disk drives attached to your computer. Under this entry, you find your hard drive and any USB drives you may have connected. If you insert a disc in your optical drive, that drive also appears. By default, Windows 7 hides empty drives.

Network

The Network entry lists all computers set up on your network.

Contents of the Selected Folder

When you click a folder on the Navigation pane, its contents appear here in the Details pane. Single-clicking the folder simply displays contents here; double-clicking the folder opens it on the Navigation pane and displays its contents here.

Context Toolbar

These toolbar buttons help you work with files and folders. They also change to meet your needs, depending on the file or folder you select.

Address Bar

The Address bar in Windows Explorer works like the Address bar in a browser. It displays the currently selected folder, and you can click the Forward and Back arrow to see other navigation paths you have already travelled.

Search Box

Using the Search text box, you can search for files and other information on your computer. Click in the Search box and type; you can filter your search by file kind, date modified, type, or name. When you filter by file kind, you filter for documents, e-mail, folders, and so on. When you filter by type, you filter by the last three or four characters of the filename, typically assigned automatically by the program that creates the file.

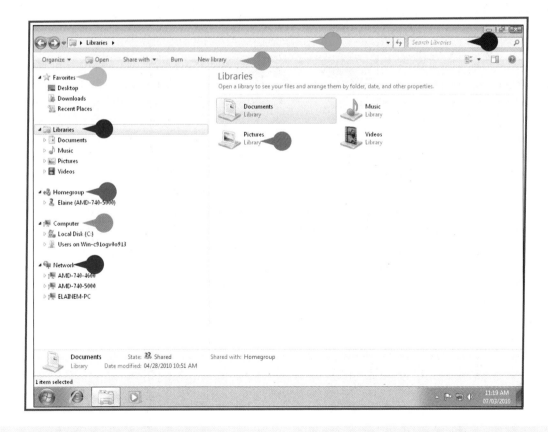

Select Files

When you work with your files to copy, move, rename, or delete them, you need to select them first. In any single folder, you can select a single file, multiple files, or a group of files. You even can select all files in a particular folder.

When you make selections, you start by selecting, in the Navigation pane, the folder

containing the files you want to select. Then, you work in the Details pane to make your selections. If you make a mistake and select a file you do not want to select, you can cancel the selection of the file.

Select Files

Select a Single File

1 In Windows Explorer, open the folder containing the file.

Note: *See the section "View Files" to open Windows Explorer.*

2 Click the file.

● Windows Explorer highlights the file you click.

Select Multiple Files

1 In Windows Explorer, open the folder containing the files.

2 Click the first file you want to select.

3 Press and hold Ctrl as you click each of the other files you want to select.

● Windows Explorer highlights the selected files.

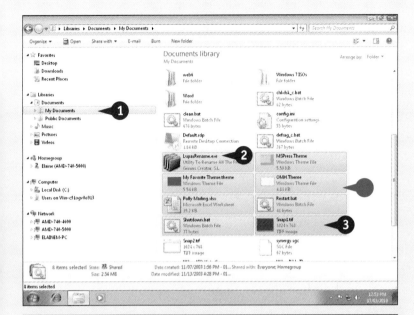

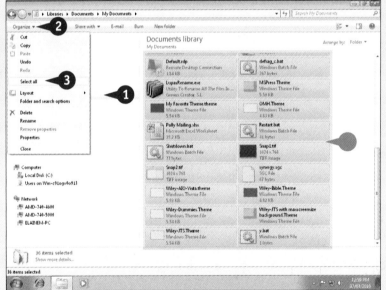

Select a Group of Files

1 In Windows Explorer, open the folder containing the files.

2 Click the first file you want to select.

3 Press and hold **Shift** as you click the last file you want to include in the selection.

● Windows Explorer highlights the first file you clicked, the last file you clicked, and all the files between them.

Select All Files

1 In Windows Explorer, open the folder containing the files.

2 Click **Organize**.

3 Click **Select all**.

● Windows Explorer selects all files in the folder.

Simplify It

How can I select all files; how can I remove a file from a multiple or group file selection?
Open the folder containing the files. Then, press and hold **Ctrl** as you press **A**. To remove files from the selection, press and hold **Ctrl** as you click the file(s) you want to remove from the selection. If you did not mean to select any files, you can cancel a selection by clicking on any white space in the folder.

Can I select a subfolder?
Yes, using the same process: click the folder containing the subfolder and then click the subfolder.

Create a New Folder

To help you organize your files, you can create new folders. Most people create folders based on subjects, but you can use any filing system you like.

Most people store their files in one of the predefined Windows 7 libraries. For example, you can create folders in the Music library for music you download from the Internet or music CDs you burn to your computer. You can create folders for pictures based on the date you took the pictures or based on the event. You might want to create a correspondence folder in the Documents library for letters you send via the U.S. Postal Service.

Create a New Folder

1 In Windows Explorer, click the folder in which you want to create a subfolder.

Note: *See the section "View Files" to open Windows Explorer.*

2 Click **New folder**.

● Windows Explorer creates a new folder called "New folder" and highlights the folder name so that you can change it.

③ Type the name you want to assign to the new folder.

④ Press Enter .

● Windows Explorer selects the new folder, and the name you assigned to the new folder appears.

Note: *By default, Windows Explorer sorts folders alphabetically followed by files alphabetically. When you press* Enter *, Windows Explorer re-sorts the folders alphabetically.*

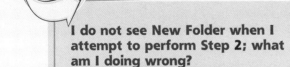

I do not see New Folder when I attempt to perform Step 2; what am I doing wrong?
You have selected one of the main headings in the Navigation pane, and you cannot create folders directly from these headings. Click a folder or entry below Favorites, Libraries, or Computer.

What happens if I create a new library?
A new entry appears below Libraries in the Navigation pane and you can use it to store files. If your computer is connected to a network, you can share that new library with other network users.

Change the Windows Explorer Layout

You can control the way Windows Explorer displays information in the Details pane using various views. For example, you can choose the Tiles view or the Details view to display the most information about each file. The Small Icons and List views display the least information about files, but more files fit on a single screen.

For pictures, the Medium Icons, Large Icons, or Extra Large Icons views show you a preview of the file's content. The Content view combines a small preview of a file's content with a small amount of file information. The Preview pane shows you content for any file type.

Change the Windows Explorer Layout

1 In Windows Explorer, open a folder.

Note: See the section "View Files" to open Windows Explorer.

Note: In this example, the open folder displays files using the Details view.

2 Click the **Views** □.

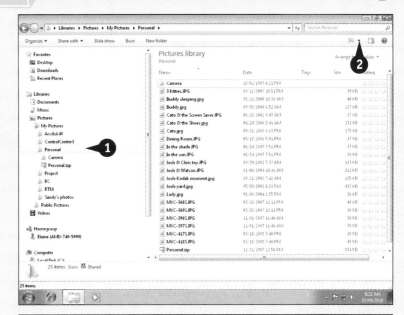

3 Click the view you want to use.

● Windows Explorer changes the Details pane to match the view you selected (in this example, the Large Icons view).

● The View slider helps you identify the view being displayed in the Details pane.

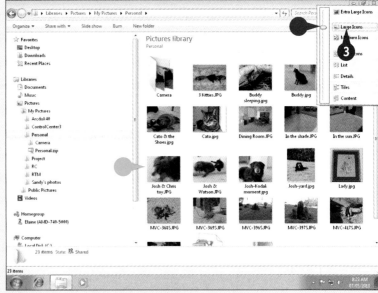

Rename a File

You can change the name of a file, which is useful if the current filename does not accurately describe the contents of the file. By giving your document a descriptive name, you make it easier to find the file later. For example, you might want to rename photos you take with a digital camera.

You should rename only those documents that you have created or that have been given to you by someone else. Do not rename any of the Windows 7 system files or any files associated with your programs; if you do rename such a file, your computer may behave erratically or even crash.

Rename a File

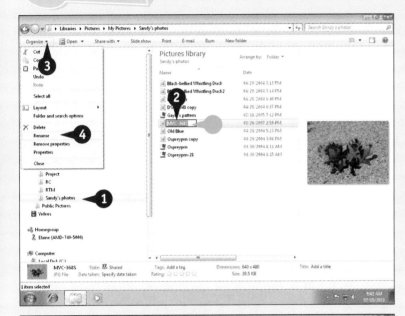

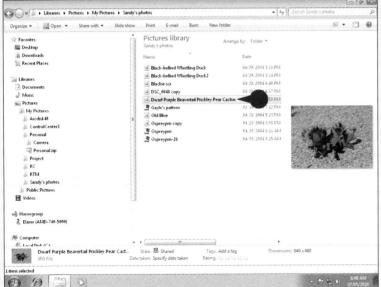

1 In Windows Explorer, open the folder that contains the file that you want to rename.

Note: See the section "View Files" to open Windows Explorer.

Note: You can also rename any folders that you have created.

2 Click the file.

3 Click **Organize**.

4 Click **Rename**.

Note: You can also select the Rename command by pressing **F2**.

● The current filename appears selected in a text box.

5 Type the new name that you want to use for the file.

Note: The name that you type can be up to 255 characters long, but it cannot include the following characters: < > , ? : " | *.

Note: If you decide that you do not want to rename the file after all, you can press **Esc** to cancel the operation.

6 Press **Enter** or click an empty section of the folder.

● Windows Explorer selects the file and displays the new filename.

Copy a File

You can make an exact copy of a file. For example, suppose that you want to place copies of photos you have taken with your digital camera on your computer's hard drive so that you can send the photos to family and friends. Or, you might want to place important files or photos on an external hard drive or a

USB flash drive to create backup copies of those files or photos.

When you copy files, the original remains in its original location and a second copy of the file appears in a location you select. You can also use this technique to copy a folder.

Copy a File

① Open the folder that contains the file that you want to copy.

Note: See the section "View Files" to open Windows Explorer.

Note: You can also copy folders; skip Step 2.

② Click the file.

Note: To copy multiple files, use the techniques described in "Select Files" earlier in this chapter.

③ Click **Organize**.

④ Click **Copy**.

Note: You can also select the Copy command by pressing Ctrl + C.

⑤ Click the folder where you want to store the copy.

⑥ Click **Organize**.

⑦ Click **Paste**.

Note: You can also select the Paste command by pressing Ctrl + V.

● A copy of the file you selected in Step 2 appears in the folder that you selected in Step 5.

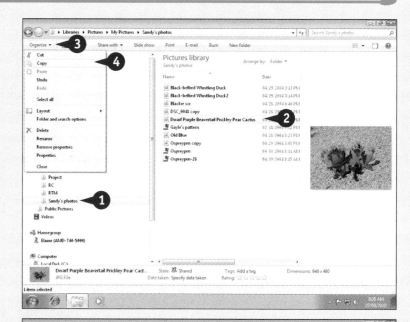

Move a File

You can move files from one folder to another; moving files deletes them from their original location and places them in a new location.

For example, you might want to move photographs from your digital camera to your computer to free up space on the digital

camera's memory card for more photographs. Or, you might decide that you want to archive certain files or photos so that they do not take up space on your computer's hard drive. You can move them to an external hard drive or a USB flash drive.

Move a File

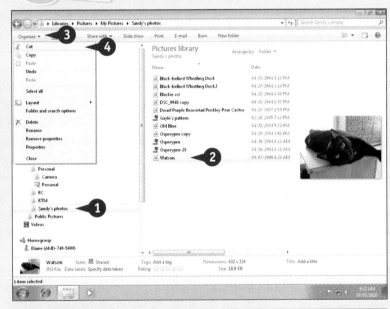

① In Windows Explorer, open the folder that contains the file that you want to move.

Note: *See the section "View Files" to open Windows Explorer.*

② Click the file.

Note: *To move multiple files, select them as described in the section "Select Files."*

③ Click **Organize**.

④ Click **Cut**.

Note: *You can also select the Cut command by pressing* Ctrl + X.

⑤ Click the folder where you want to store the copy.

⑥ Click **Organize**.

⑦ Click **Paste**.

Note: *You can also select the Paste command by pressing* Ctrl + V.

● The file you selected in Step **2** appears in the folder that you selected in Step **5** and no longer appears in the folder you opened in Step **1**.

Create a Data CD or DVD

You can create data CD or DVD that contains files by copying — or *burning* — files to the disc. You can use any type of optical media and create optical discs that you can use on any computer that uses Windows XP or later. You can add, delete, or rename files on these discs as described in this chapter.

Data CDs and DVDs are very useful for storing files you do not use regularly or need to transport. For example, you might place photos on a data CD or DVD and then take them to a drug store where you can print them. To create a music disc, see Chapter 8.

Create a Data CD or DVD

1 Insert a blank disc into your optical drive.

The AutoPlay dialog box appears.

2 Click **Burn files to disc**.

The Burn a Disc window appears.

3 Type a name for the disc here; the name can describe what you put on the disc.

4 Click **Like a USB flash drive** (◎ changes to ◉).

5 Click **Next**.

Windows 7 formats the disc and then displays the AutoPlay window.

6 Click **Open folder to view files**.

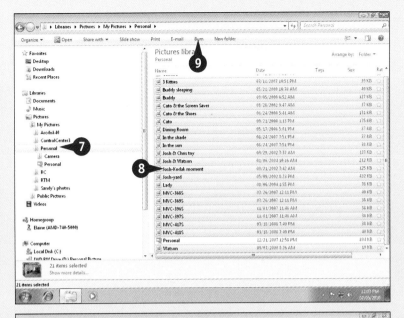

Windows Explorer opens, displaying your optical disc drive in the Navigation pane.

7 Open the folder that contains the file that you want to burn to disc.

8 Select the files.

Note: Select multiple files as described in the section "Select Files."

9 Click **Burn**.

Windows 7 burns the files to your optical drive and selects the drive in the Navigation pane.

10 Click **Close session**.

● Windows 7 displays this message as it makes the disc usable on other computers and then ejects the disc.

Does it matter whether I use a CD or DVD?
No, and it also does not matter whether you use rewritable discs. Windows 7 creates a reusable disc when it burns files. A typical DVD holds 4.7GB whereas a CD holds 650MB.

When should I choose the "With a CD/DVD player" option?
Use this option if you anticipate needing to use the disc on a computer using a Windows operating system older than Windows XP or on a computer that uses a different operating system. You cannot add, rename, or delete files stored on this type of disc.

Delete a File

When you no longer need a file, you can delete it. Deleting unwanted files helps to prevent clutter from unnecessary files on a hard drive, USB drive, or optical disc. If you accidentally delete a file, you usually can recover it; see "Restore a Deleted File" next in this chapter.

Make sure that you delete only those documents that you have created or that someone else has given to you. Do not delete any of the Windows 7 system files or any files associated with your programs; if you do, your computer may behave erratically, or even crash.

Delete a File

1 In Windows Explorer, open the folder that contains the file that you want to delete.

Note: See the section "View Files" to open Windows Explorer.

2 Click the file.

Note: To delete multiple files, select them as described in the section "Select Files."

3 Click **Organize**.

4 Click **Delete**.

Note: You can also select the Delete command when you press `Delete`.

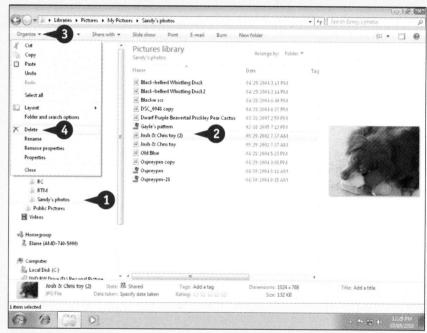

The Delete File dialog box appears.

5 Click **Yes**.

The file disappears from the folder.

Note: You can also delete a file by clicking and dragging it to the desktop's Recycle Bin icon.

If you delete a file accidentally, you can restore it. See the next section.

Restore a Deleted File

If you accidentally delete a file, you might be able to restore it to the folder where it appeared before you deleted it.

By default, Windows 7 does not completely delete a file from your computer when you delete it using the technique described in the preceding section. Instead, Windows 7 places

the file in the Recycle Bin folder, which is the equivalent of a virtual garbage can. Until you empty the Recycle Bin, you have not really deleted a file. And, because the file sits in a virtual garbage can, you can go "virtual dumpster-diving" and pull the file out of the garbage.

Restore a Deleted File

① On the Windows desktop, double-click the **Recycle Bin**.

Note: When the Recycle Bin contains files, it has the appearance of having trash in it. When the Recycle Bin contains no files, it appears to contain no trash.

Windows Explorer opens.

● The Recycle Bin folder appears in the Address bar.

● The contents of the Recycle Bin appear in the Details pane.

② In the Details pane, click the file you want to restore.

③ Click **Restore this item**.

*Note: You can use the techniques described in "Select Files" to restore multiple files simultaneously; in this case, **Restore this item** changes to **Restore the selected items**.*

The file disappears from the Recycle Bin folder and reappears in the folder from which you deleted it.

Search for a File

As you use your computer over time, you generate thousands of files, stored in various folders. At some point in time, you will not remember where you saved a particular file — or even what you called the file.

You can have Windows 7 search for your document. Windows 7 searches not only for

documents but also for applications, Internet Explorer favorites, e-mail messages, contacts, and more. And, when it searches, it searches both the filename and the content of your files. You can use two different techniques to search your computer.

Search for a File

Search from the Start Menu

① Click the **Start** button (⊞).

● The Start menu opens.

② Click here and type the word or phrase you want Windows to use when searching.

● As you type, Windows displays files that meet the search criteria, organized in groups.

To select an entry, click it; if you select a document, Windows opens the program that created the file along with the file.

To open the folder where you stored a document, right-click the document and then click **Open file location**.

To cancel the search, click outside the Start menu.

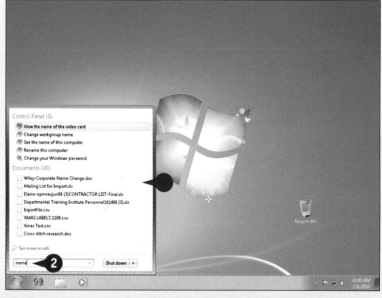

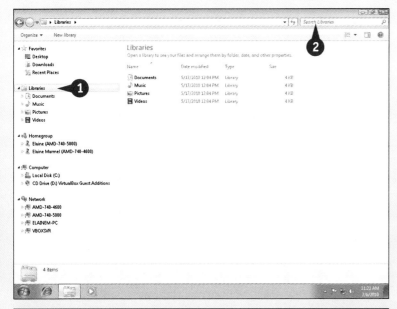

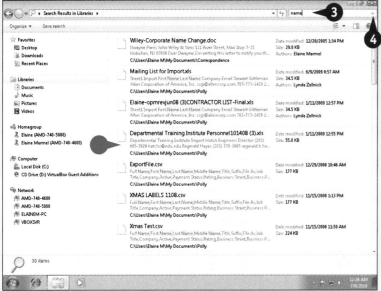

Search from Windows Explorer

1 In the Windows Explorer Navigation pane, click the location you want to search.

Note: See the section "View Files" to open Windows Explorer.

*Note: This example searches the built-in libraries. To expand a search, click a location that represents a broader search; to search your hard drive, click the **Local Disk** entry under Computer.*

2 Click in the Search text box.

3 Type the word or phrase you want Windows to use when searching.

● As you type, Windows displays files that meet the criteria in the Details pane.

Note: Each occurrence of the search phrase is highlighted.

4 To stop searching, click ⊠.

Windows redisplays your screen as it looked after Step **1**.

Simplify It

Is there a way to search for files changed on a date I specify?
Yes, you can filter search criteria. The search filters you can specify depend on the folder you select to search in the Navigation pane. For example, if you search all libraries, you can filter by filename, file kind, file type, or date modified. If you select the Pictures library, you can filter by date taken, tags, or file type. The available filters appear when you click in the Search box. To use a filter, type the filter name, a colon, and then the search criteria. To search all libraries for files changed on a specified date, click **Date Modified** in the Search box and then select the date from the calendar that appears.

Chapter 6

Securing Windows 7

Threats to your computer-related security and privacy often come from the Internet in the form of system intruders, spyware, viruses, and identity thieves. In addition, many security and privacy violations occur right at your computer by someone simply logging in to your computer while you are not around. To protect yourself and your family, you need to understand your options.

Secure Your Computer

Securing your computer means taking precautions to ensure that nobody can compromise your security or privacy. Windows 7 makes several security and privacy tools available to you.

These tools include adding a password to your account, clearing your list of recently used

documents, using the Windows 7 User Account Control feature, establishing parental controls, and taking advantage of the Windows 7 firewall and Windows Defender. In Chapters 10 and 11, you read about ways to protect yourself on the Internet and when using e-mail.

Account Password

If you share your computer with other people, create separate user accounts for each person so that each of you has your own set of files, icons, programs, and e-mail. Protecting each account with a password prevents anyone who does not know the password from logging on to the accounts. Password protection also gives you the option to lock your computer when you leave your desk so that nobody can sit down at your computer and use it to view and change files.

Clear Usage History

Windows 7 keeps track of documents and programs that you have used recently. If you know that someone else is going to be using your computer, and you do not have a separate user account set up for that person, you may not want him or her to see what is on your recent documents list. To prevent this, you can clear the list. Right-click the **Start** button (), click **Properties**, and then click **Store and display a list of recently opened files** (changes to) and **Store and display recently opened items in the Start menu and the taskbar** (changes to). You can also use a third-party program such as Privacy Guardian from PC Tools (www.pctools.com).

Confirm Actions before You Take Them

The User Account Control feature prompts you to confirm certain actions you take that could, possibly, harm your computer. If you are working from a user account configured as an administrator, you can click **Yes** to continue with the action. If you are working from a standard account, you must supply the administrator's password to continue with the action.

Parental Controls

Windows 7 offers controls that enable you to restrict the programs run by the user of a particular account. For example, you can restrict a user from running certain programs, playing certain games, or using the computer for longer than a time you specify. For details on setting parental controls, see "Establish Parental Controls" later in this chapter.

Virus and Spyware Protection

Viruses and spyware are types of malicious software that find their way onto your computer without your consent, usually via e-mail or the Internet. Windows Defender automatically runs behind the scenes of Windows 7 to protect your computer from spyware, which surreptitiously collects information about you. If you also install a good antivirus program and use a firewall, your computer will be well protected from the threats of intruders. For antivirus protection, consider Microsoft's free Security Essentials. AVG Technologies USA, Inc. offers both a free and a paid version of AVG Anti-Virus; most professionals feel the paid version works better. NOD32 from Eset is highly rated among paid versions of antivirus software.

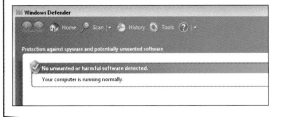

Windows 7 Firewall

Most PCs today are connected to the Internet. Because the Internet can, potentially, provide unauthorized strangers with access to your computer, you should use a firewall. Firewalls help prevent intruders from gaining access to your computer and infecting it with viruses or inflicting other damage. Windows comes with a built-in firewall that provides a basic line of defense; coupled with the firewall most routers contain, you can effectively protect your computer from unauthorized intruders. See Chapter 10 for information on the Windows 7 firewall.

Is There Such a Thing as "Too Much Security"?

Windows 7 comes with a firewall and an antispyware program. Some people feel these tools are insufficient and purchase a security suite of programs that guard against viruses, spyware, and intruders; you can find thousands of security suites by searching the Internet. Although it might seem safer to err on the side of caution and install additional security tools, these additional tools can bog down your computer's performance. Most computer professionals find that one software tool for each type of potential malware threat along with a hardware firewall provided by a router keeps you safe without impacting computer performance.

Change the Logon Password

If you assigned a password when you started Windows for the first time, you can change that password. You might want to change your password if you suspect someone has discovered it or if you think of a better password.

Assigning a password is optional but a good idea. When you protect your account with a

password, no one can log into your account unless he knows your password. If you chose not to assign a password the first time you started Windows, you can create a password for your account. Make sure you use a strong password; see the tip at the end of this section.

Change the Logon Password

① Click the **Start** button (▣).

② Click **Control Panel**.

The Control Panel window appears.

③ Click **User Accounts and Family Safety**.

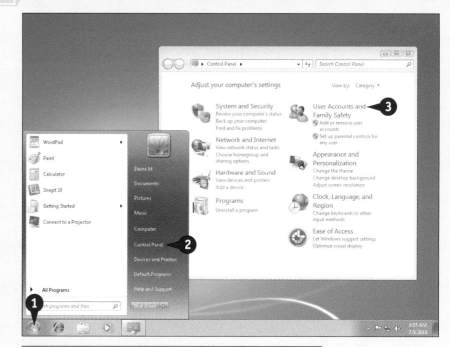

The User Accounts and Family Safety window appears.

④ Click **Change your Windows password**.

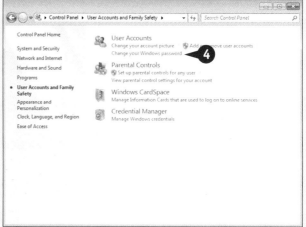

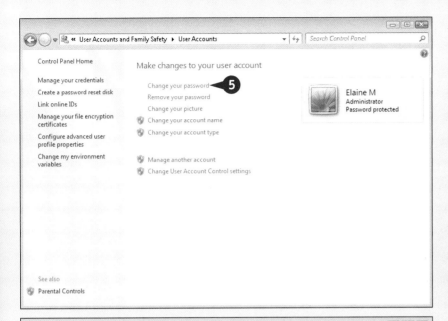

The User Accounts window appears.

⑤ Click **Change your password**.

Note: If no password currently exists for the account, click **Create a password for your account**.

The Change Your Password window appears.

⑥ Type your current password here.

Note: Windows displays substitute characters so that your password is not visible on-screen.

⑦ Type the new password you want to assign here.

⑧ Retype the new password here.

⑨ Type a hint that will remind you of the new password should you forget it.

⑩ Click **Change password**.

Windows changes your password and redisplays the User Accounts window.

⑪ Click ☒ to close the window.

Simplify It

What is a strong password?
A strong password is not obvious such as your name or "password." Additionally, it is at least eight characters long; the longer the password, the less likely someone will be able to use electronic devices to determine your password. Finally, a strong password contains at least one lowercase and one uppercase letter and one number.

Does Windows prompt for a password only when I start my computer?
No. You can lock your computer; when you attempt to unlock it, Windows prompts for your password. For more information, see "Prevent Others from Using Your Computer."

Establish Parental Controls

You can establish controls for the way children use your computer. For example, you can control the amount of time your child uses the computer, and you can control the activities in which you allow your children to participate. You can control the games you allow your children to play and the programs you allow them to run.

Windows establishes parental controls for the Windows account you select. You can allow your children to share an account, or you can establish separate accounts for each child. You must know the administrator's password or be logged on as the administrator to establish parental controls.

Establish Parental Controls

Turn On Parental Controls

1. In the Control Panel window, click **Set up parental controls for any user**.

   Note: See the section "Change the Logon Password" to open the Control Panel window.

The Parental Controls window appears.

2. Click the user account for which you want to establish parental controls.

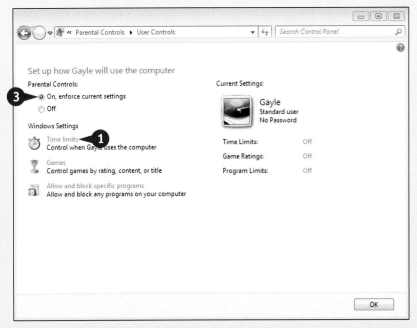

The User Controls window appears.

3 Click **On, enforce current settings** (◎ changes to ◉).

Set Time Limits

1 Click **Time limits**.

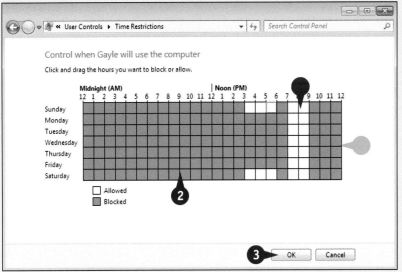

The Time Restrictions window appears.

2 Click each hour that you want to block.

● Hours you block appear in blue.

● Hours you allow access appear in white.

Note: *You can click and drag to block consecutive hours and days.*

3 Click **OK**.

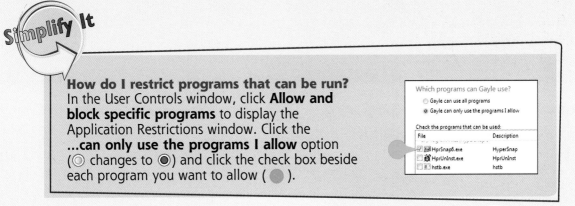

How do I restrict programs that can be run?
In the User Controls window, click **Allow and block specific programs** to display the Application Restrictions window. Click the **...can only use the programs I allow** option (◎ changes to ◉) and click the check box beside each program you want to allow (●).

Establish Parental Controls *(continued)*

When you turn on parental controls, you can set up restrictions. You can control the days of the week and the hours of those days that you permit the user access to the computer. You also can establish the maximum rating of the games you want to permit your child to play.

Windows 7 uses the Entertainment Software Rating Board system. In addition to setting a maximum rating for permitted games, you can block games with certain types of content even if the game rating falls within the maximum rating you choose to permit.

The User Controls window reappears.

Restrict Gaming

① Click **Games**.

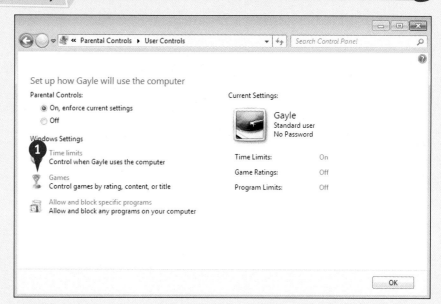

The Game Controls window appears.

② Click **Yes** (◉ changes to ◉).

Note: *To block game playing for this user, click **No**.*

③ Click **Set game ratings**.

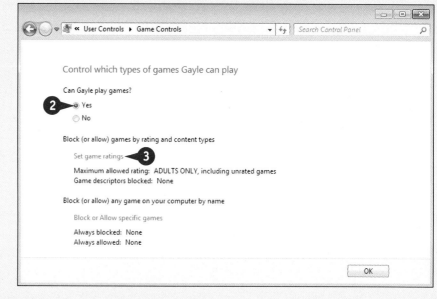

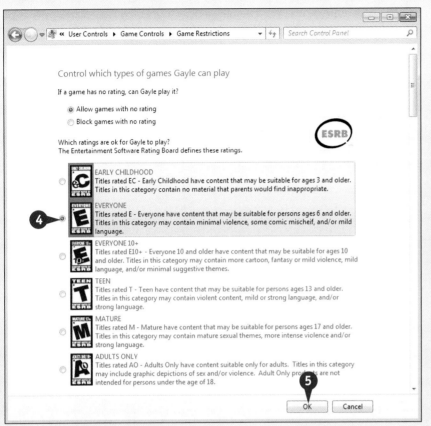

The Game Restrictions window appears.

④ Click the maximum rating you want to permit the user to play (◎ changes to ◉).

⑤ Click **OK**.

⑥ Click **OK** in the Game Controls window.

⑦ Click **OK** in the User Controls window.

⑧ Click ⊠ to close the Control Panel.

Simplify It

How do I block certain types of game content, regardless of game rating?
Reopen the Game Restrictions window and scroll down; at the bottom of the screen, you see check boxes you can select (☐ changes to ☑) to block content (●).

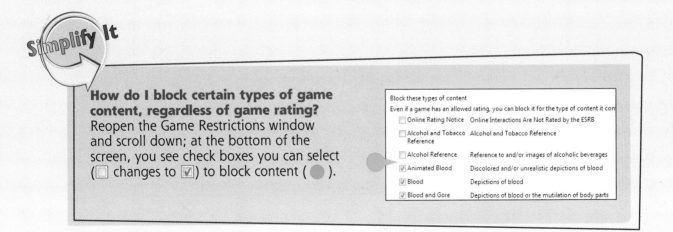

Check the Action Center

The Action Center, new to Windows 7, displays messages about the current state of your computer's security and maintenance. The Action Center focuses primarily on security issues; for example, the Action Center alerts you if updates are available for Windows 7. The Action Center also lets you know if your PC does not have virus protection installed or that protection is disabled. The Action Center notifies you if User Account Control or the Windows Firewall is disabled. And, the Action Center reminds you of tasks you need to complete, such as setting up Windows Backup.

Check the Action Center

1 In the Control Panel window, click **Review your computer's status**.

Note: See the section "Change the Logon Password" to open the Control Panel window.

The Action Center window appears.

2 Review the messages.

3 Click a button beside a message to resolve the issue.

Note: This example enables virus protection.

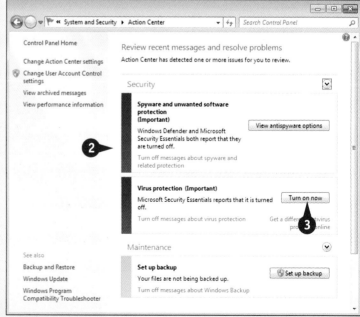

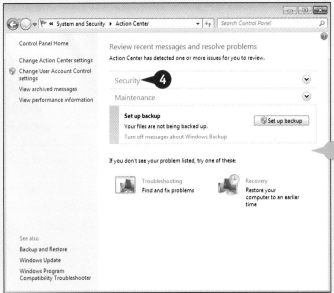

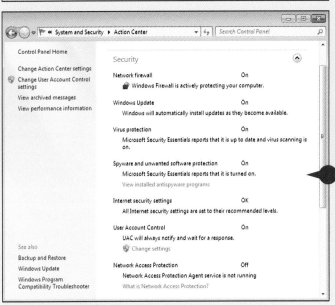

● The Action Center updates based on the actions you take.

④ Click **Security**.

● The Action Center displays a summary of the security settings on your computer.

Is there a shortcut to open the Action Center?
Yes; follow these steps. Click the Action Center flag (🏳)
in the Notifications area. A summary of Action Center
messages appears. Click **Open Action Center** to open
the Action Center window. If a security issue exists, a
small red X appears on the Action Center flag (🏳).

Prevent Others from Using Your Computer

You can require others to provide a password to use your computer at any time, not just when you turn on the computer. When you create a password for your account, Windows prompts for that password automatically when you turn on the computer and select your user account.

After you sign in to your account, your computer is available to anyone who happens to sit down at your desk. So, if you need to walk away from your computer, consider locking it first. When you lock your computer, Windows hides your desktop and displays the Welcome screen, prompting for your password.

Prevent Others from Using Your Computer

Lock Your Computer

1 Click the **Start** button (⊞).

2 Click the **Shut down** button ▶.

3 Click **Lock**.

Windows 7 locks your computer.

● On the Welcome screen, the word "Locked" appears under your user account name.

Unlock Your Computer

1 Click in the password text box.

2 Type your password.

3 Click here.

Windows 7 unlocks your computer and redisplays your desktop.

Is there an easier way to lock my computer?

You can use a keyboard shortcut; press ⊞ + Ⓛ. If you prefer to use your mouse, you can change the Shut Down button to be the Lock button; follow these steps:

1 Right-click the **Start** button (Ⓘ) and click **Properties**.

2 In the Taskbar and Start Menu Properties dialog box on the Start Menu tab, click the **Power button action** ☐.

3 Click **Lock**.

4 Click **OK**.

*Note: When you click the **Start** button (Ⓘ), "Lock" appears where "Shut down" used to appear.*

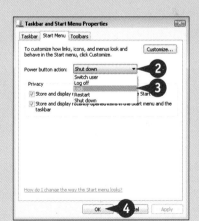

Chapter 7

Working with Software

Software programs enable you to make your computer activities more practical and fun. For example, if you want to write a letter or a memo, you can use a word processor; if you want to create a newsletter or greeting card, you can use a desktop-publishing program. This chapter shows you the basics of installing and using software programs.

Install a Program

If your computer does not come with the program that you need, you can purchase the program and then install it. You might not need to purchase the program; some vendors offer *freeware, shareware,* or *donation-ware.* Freeware is completely free; shareware is typically offered on a trial basis and might be limited in functionality or the timeframe during which you can use it. You pay an amount of your choosing for donation-ware.

How you start the installation process depends on whether you obtain the program on an optical disc or from the Internet. To be sure, look for an instruction manual or README file that comes with the program.

Install a Program

Install from a CD or DVD

1 Insert the program's CD or DVD into the optical drive.

The AutoPlay dialog box appears.

2 Click the option to run the program's setup program — typically **Run SETUP.EXE** or **Run autorun.exe**.

Note: *If the AutoPlay dialog box does not appear after you insert the disc, click the **Start** button (**), click **Computer**, and then double-click the optical drive.*

Note: *If you see the User Account Control dialog box, either click **Continue** or type an administrator password and click **Submit**.*

The software installation program begins.

3 Follow the installation instructions the program provides.

Note: *Installation steps vary from program to program.*

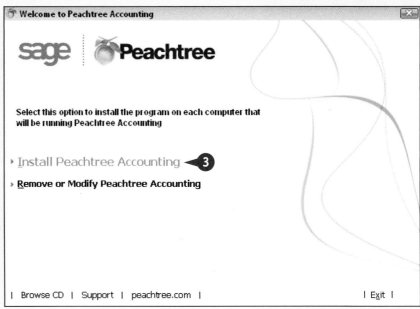

Download and Install a File from the Internet

① Navigate to the Web page that contains the download link.

② Click the download link.

The File Download – Security Warning dialog box appears.

③ Click **Save**.

What do I do if the software asks for a product key or serial number?
The product key or serial number is crucial because many programs do not install until you enter this information. Look for this number on a sticker attached to the back or inside of the CD or DVD case. You may also find it on the registration card, the disc, or the back of the box. If you download the program from the Internet, the number should appear on the download screen and on the e-mail receipt that you receive.

Peachtree Accounting 2010 Setup

Serial Number

Please enter your product serial number

Your serial number can be found on the back of the Pea
you downloaded Peachtree, you can find your serial nu

Serial Number:

Please call 1-800-388-4697 if you need assistance.

continued

Install a
Program *(continued)*

When you download a program from the Internet, it is always best to save the installation file to your computer. By saving the file, you avoid having to download the installation file again should you ever need to reinstall the program if, for example, you buy a new computer and want to install the program.

To keep your internal hard drive clean, you can copy the installation file to an external hard drive for safekeeping.

In addition, if you save the downloaded installation file on your computer, your antivirus software can check the file for viruses before you install the program.

Install a Program *(continued)*

The Save As dialog box appears.

④ Select a folder in which to store the installation file.

Note: *Many people use the Downloads folder.*

⑤ Click **Save**.

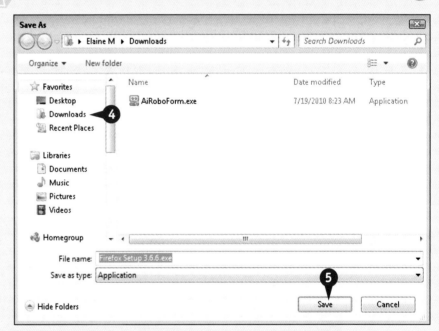

The file downloads to your computer.

When the download finishes, the Download Complete dialog box appears.

⑥ Click **Open Folder**.

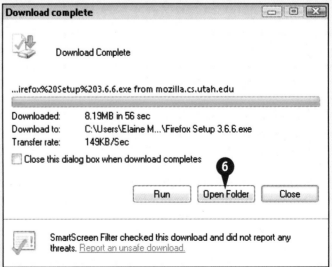

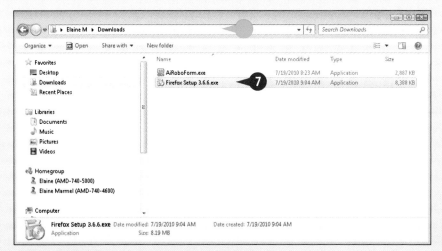

● The folder containing the installation file appears.

Note: *If you have antivirus software, you should check the downloaded file for viruses before proceeding. In most cases, you can right-click the downloaded file and then click the command that launches the antivirus check.*

❼ Double-click the downloaded file.

Either the User Account Control dialog box or the Open File – Security Warning dialog box appears.

❽ Click **Yes** or **Run**.

The software installation program begins.

❾ Follow the installation instructions the program provides.

What is the difference between a typical and custom installation?

Many programs offer two options for installation. A standard or typical installation automatically installs only those program components that the software vendor believes people use most often. If you are an inexperienced user, then you may want to choose the typical install. In a custom installation, you can select the components to install, and where to install them. The custom option is best suited for experienced users.

Uninstall a Program

When you decide to no longer use a program, you should uninstall it from your computer. Removing unused programs frees up disk space and makes your All Programs menu easier to navigate.

In addition, if you use the Custom installation option when you install a program, you can add or remove components of the program.

Some programs also give you the option to repair a program; if the program is behaving erratically, you can try repairing it if the program offers that option. If the program does not give you a "repair" option, uninstall and reinstall it.

Uninstall a Program

① Click the **Start** button (⊞).

② Click **Control Panel**.

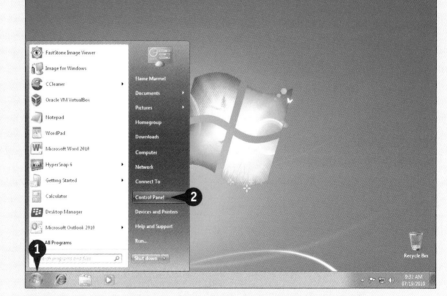

The Control Panel window appears.

③ Click **Uninstall a program**.

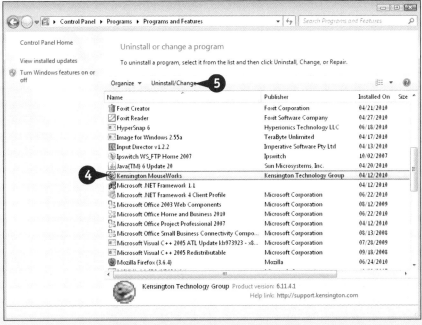

The Programs and Features window appears.

④ Click the program you want to uninstall.

⑤ Click **Uninstall** or **Uninstall/ Change**.

The program asks you to confirm that you want to uninstall it.

⑥ Click **Yes**.

The program uninstall procedure begins.

⑦ Follow the on-screen instructions, which vary from program to program.

Is there a quicker way to uninstall a program?
Possibly. Click the **Start** button (<img>), click **All Programs**, and then click the program name to open the program's folder. If you see a command that includes the word *Uninstall*, click that command to begin the uninstall procedure.

What is the difference between an automatic and a custom uninstall?
The automatic uninstall option requires no input from you. It is the easiest and safest choice, and therefore highly recommended. The custom uninstall option gives you more control, but also is more complex and should be selected only by experienced users.

Create Documents with a Word Processor

You can use word-processing software to enable you to handle your letter- and report-writing needs. Windows 7 ships with a word processor called WordPad. Other popular word processors include Microsoft Word, Corel WordPerfect, Lotus Word Pro, and the freeware Open Office Writer. Open Office Writer is part of the free Open Office productivity suite; each Open Office application closely resembles a corresponding application in older versions of Microsoft Office.

Many people use Microsoft Word. WordPad and Open Office Writer share a common file format with Microsoft Word. So, you can create documents in WordPad or Open Office Writer and share them with Word users.

Format a Document

Apply a Typeface

A typeface, also called a font, is a distinctive character set that you can apply to the selected text in a document. Most word processors have a Font list or dialog box, which you can use to choose the typeface that you want. You can change typefaces at any point in a document, but too many typefaces can make a document difficult to read.

Change Font Size

The font size refers to the height and width of each character, measured in points; 72 points equal one inch. Use a larger font size for section headings and headlines. Use a standard font size — typically 11 or 12 point — for regular text in a document.

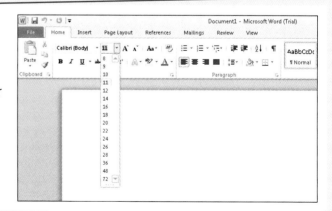

Black-Bellied Whistling Duck

The *black-bellied whistling duck* can be found in streams and ponds southern Arizona, resides in southern Texas, and has been introduced in Flo

Physical Characteristics

Generally, 20-22", the black-bellied whistling duck is a large, long-le adult has a bright orange bill, pink legs, a gray face and upper neck with whi a chestnut cap, nape, lower neck, chest and back, and a black belly. White s bases to the black primary and secondary coverts create a long wing stripe i patch at rest.

Apply Text Effects

Text effects change the appearance of the text to call the reader's attention to it. The most common examples are **bold**, *italics*, underline, and ~~strikethrough~~ (B, I, U, and abc). In most word processors, you can apply effects either by using the Font dialog box or by using buttons.

Format a Paragraph

You can format a paragraph in several ways. For example, you can align text with the left or right margin, or center it between the margins. You also can indent a paragraph from the left or right margin, or you can indent just the first line. You can adjust the spacing between lines within the paragraph and between paragraphs.

Declaration of Independence

When in the Course of human events, it becomes necessary for one pe bands which have connected them with another, and to assume amon separate and equal station to which the Laws of Nature and of Nature' respect to the opinions of mankind requires that they should declare t to separation.

We hold these truths to be self-evident, that all men are create endowed by their Creator with certain Unalienable Rights, tha and the pursuit of Happiness. That to secure these rights, gove among Men, deriving their just powers from the consent of the

That whenever any form of Government becomes destructive of these People to alter or to abolish it and to institute a new Government, layi

---

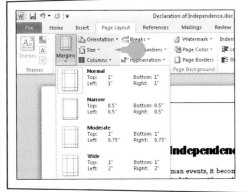

Format a Page

Formatting the page usually involves setting three basic features: the paper size, such as letter or legal; the margin sizes; and the page orientation (⬤). Page orientations include portrait, where the text runs across the short side of the page, and landscape, where the text runs across the long side of the page.

continued

Create Documents with a Word Processor *(continued)*

Add Numbering or Bullets

Most word processors enable you to format a list of items in a way appropriate to the list's content. For example, if the list is a sequence of steps, you can format it as a numbered list. Or, if you have a list of items that can appear in a random order, you can use a bulleted list.

Aunt Abigail's Helpful Hints

Do you have any of the following stains on your carpet?

- Alcohol
- Blood
- Wine
- Cigarette burns
- Stains from pets

Don't worry. *Aunt Abigail's Helpful Hints* contains tips and tricks you can use to clean up these stains and more. This amazing pamphlet-style book will help you make your carpet look like nobody has ever used it.

Add Images

Word-processing documents are mostly text, but you can also insert images such as digital photos, clip art, scanned pictures, or artwork that you create. Images add variety and interest to a document and can complement the text by illustrating concepts or showing examples.

Black-Bellied Whistling Duck

The *black-bellied whistling duck* can be found in streams southern Arizona, resides in southern Texas, and has been introd

Physical Charact

Generally
duck is a large, lo
has a bright oran
neck with white
cap, nape, lower
White secondary
primaries and se
flight and a visibl

Find and Replace Text

All word processors have a Find feature that enables you to search a document for a word or phrase. Word processors also come with a Replace feature that complements the Find feature; using the Replace feature you can find specific text and then replace it with different text.

Perfect a Document

Choose Synonyms and Antonyms

The more powerful word processors come with a collection of writing tools that enable you to perfect your prose. Using the thesaurus, you can enter a word and the program provides you with one or more synonyms as well as antonyms. You can then pick the synonym or antonym that best conveys your meaning and insert it in your document.

Check Spelling

Few things can mar your document as much as spelling mistakes. If other people read your documents, your word processor should include a spell-checking feature. Typically, this feature automatically checks each word for the proper spelling, suggests alternatives if it finds a mistake, and enables you to quickly fix the error.

Physical Characteristics

Generally, 20-22", the black-bellied whistling duck is a large, long-legged, long-necked duck. The adult has a bright orange bill, pink legs, a gray face and upper neck with white eye ring. This duck sports a chestnut cap, nape, lower neck, chest and back, and a black belly. White secondary coverts and white bases to the black primaries and secondaries create a long wing stripe in flight and a visible pale patch at rest.

which have connected them with another, and to assume among the powers of the earth, equal station to which the Laws of Nature and of Nature's God entitle them, a decent resp of mankind requires that they should declare the causes which impel them to separation.

We hold these truths to be self-evident, that all men are created equal, that they a their Creator with certain Unalienable Rights, that a hese are life, Liberty Ha — . That to secure these rights, governments are instituted among Men, c powers from the consent of the governed,

That whenever any form of Government becomes destructive of these ends, it is the right

Check Grammar

Grammar mistakes can be just as jarring as spelling mistakes, and so a good word processor should check your grammar. This feature looks for errors such as subject-verb agreement, capitalization, sentence fragments, and punctuation ( ). Typically, grammar checkers tell you why selected text is problematic but do not make suggestions to correct the problems.

Crunch Numbers with a Spreadsheet

A spreadsheet is a software program that enables you to work with numbers in rows and columns and apply formulas to the numbers to quickly create powerful mathematical, financial, and statistical models.

Windows 7 does not come with a spreadsheet. Popular spreadsheet programs include Microsoft Excel, Corel Quattro Pro, and Lotus 1-2-3. The freeware Open Office productivity suite contains Calc, a spreadsheet application that closely resembles older versions of Microsoft Excel. Many people use Microsoft Excel, and Excel and Open Office Calc share a common file format. So, you can create documents in Open Office Calc and share them with Excel users.

Spreadsheet Basics

Row

In a spreadsheet program, each horizontal row has a unique number that identifies it; the number appears to the left of the row. For example, the topmost row is 1, the next row is 2, and so on. As spreadsheet programs have advanced, the number of rows available to you has increased.

Column

Each vertical column in a spreadsheet has a unique letter that identifies it. For example, the leftmost column is A, and the next column is B. Again, as spreadsheet programs have advanced, the number of columns available to you has increased.

Cell

A cell is the term used to refer to the box in which you enter your data. A cell appears at the intersection of a row and a column.

Cell Address

You refer to a cell by its cell address, which is made up of the intersecting column letter and row number at the cell's location, and you always state the column letter before the row number. For example, the cell in the sixth column and third row of a spreadsheet is referred to as F3 because it appears at the intersection of column F and row 3. In Excel, the cell address appears above column letters.

Range

A range is a rectangular grouping of two or more cells. The range address is given by the address of the top left cell and the address of the bottom right cell. F11:H14 is an example of a range of cells.

Build a Spreadsheet

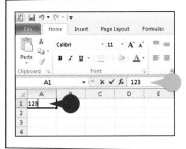

Add Data

You can insert text, numbers, and other characters into any cell in the spreadsheet. Click the cell in which you want to enter information and then type. When you are done, press **Enter**. Your typing appears in the cell that you selected (●) and in the formula bar (●). To edit existing cell data, click the cell and then edit the text in the formula bar.

Add a Formula

A formula is a collection of numbers, cell addresses, and mathematical operators that performs a calculation. In most spreadsheets, you enter a formula in a cell by typing **=** and then the formula text. For example, the formula =B2-A2 subtracts the value in cell A2 from the value in cell B2. The result appears in the cell (●), whereas the formula appears in the formula bar (●).

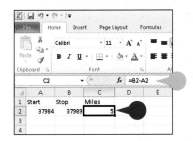

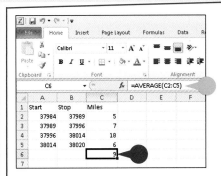

Add a Function

A function is a predefined formula that performs a specific task. For example, the AVERAGE function calculates the average of a list of numbers, and the PMT function calculates a loan or mortgage payment. You can use functions on their own, preceded by = , or as part of a larger formula. The result appears in the cell (●), whereas the formula appears in the formula bar (●).

continued

Crunch Numbers with a Spreadsheet *(continued)*

Calculate Totals Quickly

If you need a sum of a list of numbers, use the SUM function. Click a cell below the numbers and then click the **AutoSum** button (Σ), which is available in most spreadsheets. In some spreadsheets, such as Excel, you can select the cells that you want to sum, and their total, along with other common calculations, appears in the status bar ( ).

Fill a Series

Most spreadsheet programs enable you to save time by completing a series of values automatically. For example, if you need to enter consecutive dates in consecutive cells, you can enter just the first few dates, select the cells, and then click and drag the lower right corner to fill in the rest of the numbers. Most programs also fill in numbers, as well as the names for weekdays and months.

Manage Tables

The row-and-column format of a spreadsheet makes the program suitable for simple databases called tables (or lists). Each column becomes a field in the table, and each row is a record. You can sort the records, filter the records to show only certain values, and add subtotals.

Enhance a Spreadsheet

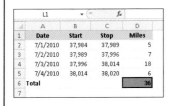

Format Cells

All spreadsheet programs enable you to format cells and ranges to make your work more attractive and effective. You can format text with fonts, effects, sizes, and colors, add a border around a cell, change the background color of a cell, and align text. You can format numbers using a variety of number styles, such as comma or currency, which includes a dollar sign ($).

Change Row and Column Sizes

The default column widths and row heights are not fixed. You can adjust the widths and heights to fit your cell data or to create special effects. To change the column width in most spreadsheets, you simply click and drag the right edge of the column header (●). To change the row height, you can click and drag the bottom edge of the row header.

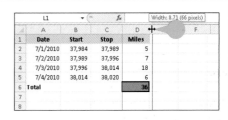

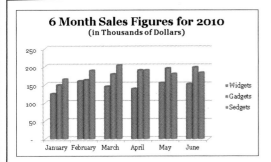

Add a Chart

A chart is a graphic representation of spreadsheet data. As the data in the spreadsheet changes, the chart also changes to reflect the new numbers. Most spreadsheet programs support a wide variety of charts, including bar charts, line charts, and pie charts.

Build Presentations with a Presentation Program

A presentation program enables you to build professional-looking slides that you can use when making a presentation to convey your ideas to other people.

Windows 7 does not come with a presentation program. Other popular presentation programs include Microsoft PowerPoint, Corel Presentations, and Lotus Freelance Graphics. The freeware Open Office productivity suite contains Impress, a presentation application that closely resembles older versions of Microsoft PowerPoint. Many people use Microsoft PowerPoint, and PowerPoint and Open Office Impress share a common file format. So, you can create documents in Open Office Impress and share them with PowerPoint users.

Presentation Basics

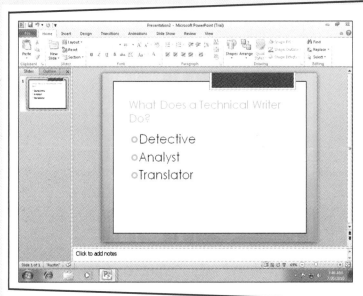

Slide

A presentation consists of slides. Each slide is a single screen that can contain your text, images, and other data. A slide usually deals with only a single topic from your presentation, and you display just the topic basics — often in point form — while you expand on the topic in your talk.

Slide Show

A slide show consists of a collection of slides in a presentation, as well as details such as the transitions between slides, slide animation effects, and narration. You can present the slide show on your computer, on the Internet, on a CD, or project it onto a screen.

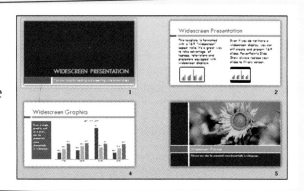

Build a Presentation

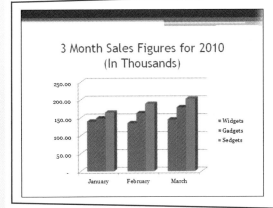

Add Content

Most slides contain text, which usually consists of a slide title followed by several bulleted points. However, most presentation programs also enable you to enhance your slides with tables and nontext content such as charts, images, clip art, and even multimedia files such as sound clips and videos.

Format the Slides

All presentation programs enable you to format your slides for maximum readability and impact. You can format text with fonts, effects, and colors. You can change font size and spacing. You also can change the paragraph spacing and text alignment, and add a shape.

Add Themes, Animations, and Transitions

You can change how the slide content appears. For example, you can add a theme to your presentation that appears on all slides. And, you can use animation to show only one bullet at a time. You can also change the transition from one slide to another. For example, you can fade the current slide out and fade the next slide in.

Run the Slide Show

Most presentation programs give you a great deal of flexibility for setting up the slide show. For example, you can choose to advance the slides manually by clicking the mouse, or automatically at a defined interval. You can loop the slides, and turn narration on and off.

Store Information with a Database

A database program enables you to store, manipulate, and view large quantities of related data. The simplest example of a database is the telephone book, which contains address and telephone information for each listed name.

Windows 7 does not ship with a database. Other popular databases include Microsoft

Access, Corel Paradox, and Lotus Approach. The freeware Open Office productivity suite contains Base, a presentation application that closely resembles older versions of Microsoft Access. Many people use Microsoft Access, and Access and Open Office Base share a common file format. So, you can create databases in Open Office Base and share them with Access users.

Database Basics

Table

A table is where you store your data. Each table is a collection of related information, such as a list of employees, products, orders, or recipes, and most database files consist of multiple tables. Each table consists of multiple records.

Record

A record is a collection of related information about one item in the table. For example, in an employee table, the information about each employee would be a record. Records appear across rows in the database table.

Field

A field is one element of information in a record. For example, in an employee record, the employee's last name is a field. Other fields could include the employee's first name, job title, birth date, and hire date. Fields appear in columns in the database table.

Field Name

Each field in a table has a unique name to identify it. Field names appear in the first row of the table.

Work with Data

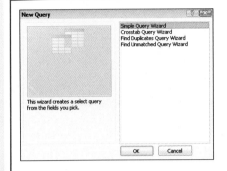

Query Data

A query is a method for extracting information from a table by applying specific conditions, called criteria, to the data. For example, in a table of customer sales data, you can create a query to display the top ten non-U.S. customers.

Enter Data with a Form

All databases rely on having accurate, timely information, and so it is extremely important to enter data efficiently and correctly. To help you do this, all database programs allow you to design forms for data entry. A form is a screen that usually presents one record at a time. The design of the form makes entering data easier.

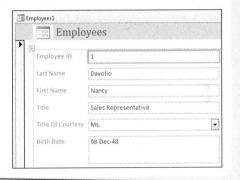

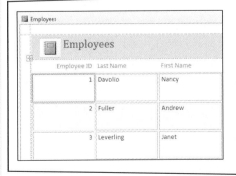

View Data in a Report

A report is a summary of the data contained in a table or a query. You can format the report to present the data attractively and effectively, and most database programs allow you to supplement the report with subtotals and other calculations.

Manipulate Pictures
with an Image Editor

You can use your computer to create, view, and manipulate pictures, drawings, digital photos, scanned images, screenshots, and other types of graphic files. Using a drawing program, you can create images and make basic edits. Image editors contain more extensive editing tools.

Windows 7 ships with a drawing program called Paint. The freeware Open Office productivity suite includes Draw, a drawing program comparable to Microsoft Visio, with more extensive drawing capabilities than Paint. The freeware Windows Live Essentials, available from Microsoft, contains an image-editing program called Photo Gallery. Other popular image editors include Adobe Photoshop and Corel PaintShop Photo Pro.

Obtain Images

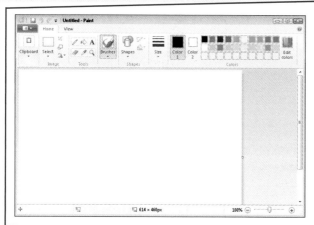

Create Images

Drawing and painting programs enable you to create your own images. You can use a drawing program for relatively simple line drawings, and you can use a painting program for more elaborate works. Both types of programs offer a number of tools for creating shapes, drawing freehand, and applying colors.

Import Images

All image editors enable you to open existing image files stored on your computer. If the image you want is stored on a digital camera or exists on paper, most image editors can acquire the image from the camera or a document scanner.

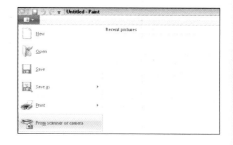

Work with Images

Manipulate Images

Once you open the image in an image editor, the program offers a number of methods for manipulating the image. For example, you can change the size, crop out parts that you do not need, and flip or rotate the image.

Enhance Photos

The better image editors include a number of tools that enable you to retouch and enhance your photos. For example, you can remove red eye, adjust the color balance and contrast, and sharpen the image.

Add Effects

Most image editors also enable you to add special effects to an image. For example, you can take a color photo — even a digital photo — and make it look like it was taken with black-and-white film.

Create Publications with a Desktop-Publishing Program

A desktop-publishing program enables you to compose professional-looking publications that combine text and images. For example, you can create flyers, brochures, greeting cards, catalogs, newsletters, and letterheads.

Windows 7 does not come with any built-in desktop-publishing programs. And, major freeware applications such as Open Office and Windows Live Essentials do not include desktop-publishing programs. Popular desktop publishers include Microsoft Publisher, Adobe InDesign, and QuarkXPress. You can download a free trial of Microsoft Publisher as part of a trial version of Office 2010 Professional. You can purchase Microsoft Publisher separately if you do not want the other programs in the Office suite.

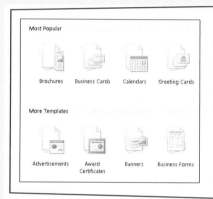

Choose a Publication Type

Your first step with a desktop-publishing program is to choose the type of publication that you want to compose. Most desktop-publishing programs offer a number of publication types. These types add a number of design elements automatically, which is easier than creating the entire document yourself.

Choose a Design

Once you have chosen your publication type, your next step is to choose an overall design for the publication, which includes text formatting, page layout, and graphic accent elements. Choosing a design saves you from having to construct these items yourself.

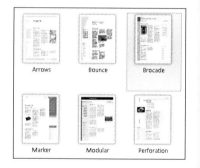

Add or Edit Text

Prefabricated publications contain text placeholders that say things like "Newsletter Title," "Name of Recipient," and "Business Name." Click these placeholders and type the text that you want. To add new text, you insert a text box and type your text in the box.

Add Images

All desktop-publishing programs enable you to add image files to your publication, either as new images or as replacements for images in the prefabricated designs.

Click and Drag

Once all of your publication elements are on the page, you can adjust the page layout to maximize the attractiveness and effectiveness of the publication. Each text box and image on the page is a separate item that you can click and drag with your mouse to move to the appropriate location.

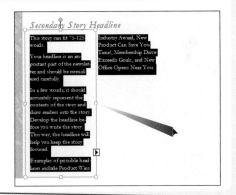

Review

All desktop-publishing programs enable you to check the spelling and grammar in your publication. Using these tools, you can avoid embarrassing moments and save money by catching these types of mistakes before you print or mail your publication.

Chapter 8

Using Multimedia

You can use a combination of software and hardware to play, view, and edit a wide variety of multimedia. For example, you can use your computer to listen to sounds and music, and view photos, drawings, videos, and animations.

How Digital Cameras Work

You can use a digital camera to take photos that the camera stores internally on a memory card. You can then connect the camera to your computer and transfer some or all of the photos to your hard drive.

You can use a digital video camera — also called a *camcorder* — to record videos that the camera stores internally. You can then connect the video camera to your computer and transfer the video to your computer for editing and for transfer to a DVD.

Megapixels

One of the most important features of a digital still or video camera is the number of megapixels, which measures the detail in each photo. A megapixel represents a million pixels. (See the section "Discover Digital Images" to learn more about pixels.) The number of megapixels affects the quality of the image and the image size you can print; the more megapixels, the better the picture.

Digital Camera Memory

All digital cameras have some form of internal memory — usually in the form of a memory card, such as a CompactFlash card — that they use to store the photos that you take. If you take a photo that you do not like, you can delete it from memory and try again. The amount of memory affects the number of photos that the camera can store internally, and so the more memory the camera has, the more photos it can store.

Digital Video Camera Storage

Like their still-picture cousins, digital video cameras store your video footage internally until you are ready to transfer the footage to your computer. Digital video cameras use a wide variety of storage devices, including memory cards, optical disks, and hard drives. Older digital video cameras store video footage on cassette tapes.

Features

Today's digital cameras and digital video cameras come with many of the features found in film cameras, including built-in flashes and zoom lenses. These cameras also come with LCD screens, and many digital still cameras can also capture short video sequences.

Transfer Photos

When you are ready to work with your photos, you can transfer them to your computer using either of two techniques. You can remove the camera's memory card and insert it in the memory card reader attached to your computer. Or, you can connect your digital camera to your computer using a USB cable and use the software that came with the camera to transfer the images to your computer. When the transfer is complete, delete the images from the camera so that you can store new photos.

Transfer Videos

The method you use to transfer videos to your computer depends on the storage method of the camera. For example, if the camera uses optical discs, you remove the disc from the camera and insert it in your optical drive. If your camera uses memory cards, you can remove them from the camera and insert them in your computer's memory card reader, or you can connect your digital video camera to your computer using a USB cable.

How Webcams Work

You can use a webcam to capture live photos directly to your computer or to an Internet site. The webcam captures photos at intervals you specify and then stores them on your computer. Many webcams capture video as well as still photos, and you can use a webcam in a video conversation.

You can also use a webcam to record live video for use in video e-mails. A video e-mail is an e-mail message that includes a video captured by a webcam as an attachment. Video e-mail is a convenient way to share short home movies with friends or family.

Live Photos

Most webcams come with special software that enables you to capture live photos at regular intervals. You can then send each new photo to your Web site to create a constantly updated view of a scene or object. Most webcam software also enables you to send a photo through e-mail.

Live Video

Many webcams can also capture live video. For example, the San Diego Zoo displays their "Panda Cam" live video of the Giant Panda exhibit; they use a webcam to stream the activities of the pandas over the Internet. They also have a Polar Cam, an Elephant Cam, and an Ape Cam, so, you can go to the zoo while you sit at your computer. To watch their live video cams, visit www.sandiegozoo.org.

Video Conversation

A video conversation, or *video chat*, is an Internet-based form of communication in which two people can both see and hear each other. To have a video conversation, both parties need a webcam, a sound card, speakers, and a microphone. Many webcams have built-in microphones, and software such as Windows Messenger enables you to have a live video chat.

Site Monitoring

A webcam is a useful tool for monitoring a site. For example, you could enhance the security of your home or office by using a webcam to monitor a live feed of your front door or a secure area. Similarly, many parents use webcams to monitor toddlers and children. Some webcams have built-in motion sensors, so that they transmit video only when they detect movement. You can find steps for setting up your webcam as a security tool at www.simplehelp.net. On the site, search for "webcam security."

How Digital Audio Players Work

You can use a digital audio player, also called an *MP3 player*, to store and play digital music files. Digital audio players are small, lightweight, and sturdy, so you can listen to music while walking, jogging, or performing errands. Popular digital audio players include the Apple iPod, the Microsoft Zune, the

SanDisk Sansa, the Creative Zen Vision, and the Toshiba Gigabeat.

You can synchronize media on your computer with media on your digital audio player using software. For example, you use iTunes, a free utility that you download from the Internet, to synchronize media on your computer and media on an iPod.

Storage

Most digital audio players store music files internally using flash memory chips that allow for quick recording and erasing of files. The flash memory is built either into the player or on removable memory cards. Some players, such as the Apple iPod and the Microsoft Zune, have internal hard drives. Most players support at least two music file formats: MP3 and WMA. For more about these file types, see "Understanding Digital Audio."

Features

Digital audio players range from simple devices that only play music to more complex devices that show pictures and videos. Many players have FM tuners that enable you to listen to FM radio. Other players have built-in microphones for voice recording. For walking or jogging with your player, you might need either an arm strap or a belt clip.

Access Music

You place music onto your digital audio player either by buying the music from the Internet or by transferring audio tracks from your computer. Most digital audio players connect to the computer through a USB cable. The players also use software that enables you to organize your music files and send them to the player, and the software you use depends on the digital audio player you use.

Understanding Digital Images

A digital image is any picture that exists in an electronic format, including photos, drawings, scanned pictures, and clip art. You can create digital drawings and clip art using drawing software; you also can find many free clip art images on the Internet. You can create digital photos with a digital camera or by scanning a print. Once you have digital images on your computer, you can incorporate them into presentations, reports, e-mail messages, and Web pages.

To understand how to work with digital images, you need to learn a few fundamental concepts. For example, you should understand pixels, image resolution, color quality, image compression, and file formats.

Pixels

A *pixel*, short for *picture element*, is a tiny square of light on your screen. Everything you see on your computer is displayed by changing the colors of individual pixels. A typical screen can have anywhere from 480,000 to nearly 2 million pixels, arranged in a row-and-column grid.

Resolution

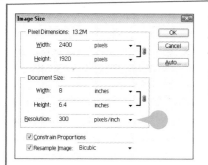

The image resolution is given by the density of the pixels in the image. The higher the resolution — that is, the higher the pixel density — the sharper the image. Image resolution is measured in pixels per inch, or PPI (●). Typical values are 75, 150, and 300 PPI.

Color Quality

The color quality, also called the *bit depth*, measures how much color information is available to display or print each pixel in an image. Higher color quality means a more accurate representation of colors in a digital image but also a larger file size for the image. For example, a pixel with a bit depth of 1 has two possible values: black and white. Common color-quality values are 256 colors (also called 8-bit color), 65,536 colors (16-bit), and 16 million colors (24-bit).

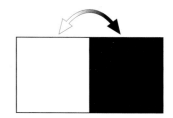

Work with Images

You can use image-editing software to view and edit your digital images. For example, you can change the image size, crop out elements that you do not want, or add special effects. You can print the photos on a color or photo printer, or you can have a store print them for you.

Image Compression

To make large digital files easier to manipulate, most images are compressed to a certain extent to make them smaller. Some formats use lossy compression, which removes redundant or unneeded pixels in the image. Other formats use lossless compression, which maintains the integrity of the original image. In general, lossy compression generates smaller but poorer-quality files than files generated by lossless compression.

File Formats

You can save digital image files in a variety of formats, each of which has its own features and advantages. For example, BMP (bitmap) images use lossless compression and are good for color drawings. JPEG images use lossy compression, and the resulting small files are good for uploading to a Web site or sending through e-mail. TIFF images use lossless compression and are good for rendering photos and scanned images.

```
JPG - JPEG Image
MHT - Web Page with Imac
PDF - Adobe PDF
PNG - Portable Network Gr
SNAG - Snagit Capture File
SWF - Adobe Flash
TIF - Tagged Image File
```

Understanding Digital Video

A digital video is a series of consecutive pictures that produce a moving image that exists in an electronic format. Examples of digital video include files transferred from a digital video camera, live feeds from a webcam, DVD movies, and animations. Once you have digital videos on your computer, you can incorporate them into presentations, e-mail messages, and Web pages.

Understanding digital videos requires that you learn about a few fundamental concepts, such as frame rates, video size, video compression, and video file formats.

Frame Rate

The frame rate measures the number of still images, or frames, that a digital video file displays every second. The frame rate is measured in frames per second (fps). The higher the frame rate, the smoother the motion appears in the digital video; however, this results in a larger file and the need for more processing power. The two most common frame rates for digital video are 30 fps (full-motion video), which produces smooth motion, and 15 fps, which produces jerky motion.

Video Size

The video size measures the dimensions — the width and height — of the video frames, expressed in pixels. For example, a 320×240-pixel video has frames that are 320 pixels in width and 240 pixels in height. The greater the video size, the larger the file size, and the more processing power required to play the file. The most common digital video sizes are 320×240, 640×480, and 720×480, also called *full-screen video*.

Work with Videos

After you transfer the video to your computer, you can use video-editing software to view and edit the video. Windows 7 offers Windows Movie Maker, a very basic video-editing software package, and third-party products such as Adobe Premier and Roxio Creator are also available. You can rearrange clips, add sound effects, and insert transitions between scenes.

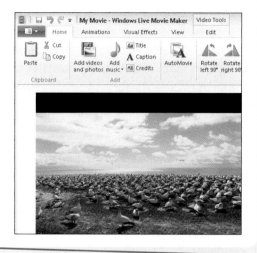

Video Compression

Digital video files can be huge, and so some compression is required to make the files easier to use. All digital video recorder compression formats use lossy compression, which removes redundant or unneeded portions of the video. For example, the compression may record only the data that changes from one frame to another, rather than entire frames.

File Formats

You can save digital video files in a variety of formats, each of which has its own features and advantages. The most common format is MPEG (Motion Picture Experts Group), which uses lossy compression and has three main standards: MPEG-1, which produces near-VHS-quality video; MPEG-2, which produces DVD-quality video; and MPEG-4, which is an enhanced version of MPEG-2 that produces even smaller files. WMV (Windows Media Video) is similar to MPEG-4, but produces even smaller files. AVI files are limited to 320×240 pixels at 30 fps, but are supported by all versions of Windows.

Understanding Digital Audio

Digital audio is any sequence of sounds that exists in electronic format, including music, audio CDs, sound effects, recorded sounds, and the narration or sound track that accompanies a digital video. Once you have digital audio on your computer, you can listen to it as well as incorporate it into presentations, digital video projects, and Web pages.

Understanding digital audio requires that you learn about a few fundamental concepts, such as digital sampling, bit rates, MP3s and other audio file formats, and music licensing.

Digital Sampling

Digital sampling is the process by which an analog sound wave is converted into a digital format. A *sample* is a snapshot of the sound wave at a given moment. The sample is a measurement of the wave's height (its loudness or amplitude), and these measurements are taken at discrete intervals to form a digital approximation of the original wave.

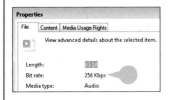

Bit Rate

The *bit rate*, also spelled *bitrate*, measures the digital sampling rate used to create a digital audio file. Bit rate is measured in thousands of bits per second (Kbps) (●). Although a higher bit rate results in a better sound quality, it also results in a larger file. For example, a digital audio file sampled at 128 Kbps (called near-CD quality) sounds better than one sampled at 64 Kbps (called FM radio quality), but the resulting file is twice as large.

MP3s

The Motion Picture Experts Groups Audio Level 3, or MP3, is one of the most popular audio file formats. It compresses digital audio by removing extraneous sounds that the human ear does not normally detect. This process results in high-quality audio files that are one-tenth the size of uncompressed audio, thus making MP3s ideal for downloading and storing on digital audio players (frequently called MP3 players, even when they support other audio formats).

Other File Formats

Besides MP3, digital audio comes in a number of other file formats. The most popular of these is Windows Media Audio (WMA), which produces audio files with the same quality as MP3, but that are compressed to about half the size. WMA is often used for digital audio player storage because it can fit twice the number of songs as MP3. The WAV format is supported by all Windows versions, but it is uncompressed and so is suitable for only short sound effects or snippets. Less popular audio formats are MIDI, AIFF, and AU.

MPEG-4 Audio (*.m4a)
GSM (*.gsm)
Dialogic Vox (*.vox)
Raw Audio (*.raw)
RSS Podcast Audio (*.rss)
M3U Playlist File (*.m3u)
PLS Playlist File (*.pls)
WPL Playlist File (*.wpl)
AMR Narrowband Audio (*.amr)
Musepack Audio (*.mpc)
Monkey's Audio Codec (*.ape)
Speex (*.spx)
Wave (*.wav)

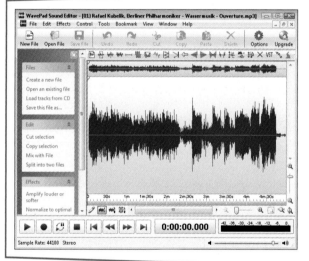

Work with Digital Audio

You can use audio-editing software to play and edit your digital audio. For example, you can delete portions of the file, change the volume or speed, and add special effects. You can also use some audio-editing programs to record sounds through a microphone or from an external audio source such as a turntable, cassette player, or digital audio tape player.

Digital Audio Licenses

Some digital audio content is in the public domain, which means that you can use it without paying for it. However, most digital audio content — particularly commercial music — is protected by copyright. This means that legally you should not play the audio unless you get permission or pay a fee. In either case, you are given a digital license (●) that allows you to play the audio file, and that may also place restrictions on whether you can copy the file to devices other than your computer.

Enhanced Playback and Device Experience
☑ Display media information from the Internet
☑ Update music files by retrieving media info from the Internet
☑ Download usage rights automatically when I play or sync a file
☑ Automatically check if protected files need to be refreshed
☑ Set clock on devices automatically

Copy Music CD Tracks to Your Computer

You can copy tracks from a music CD to your computer's hard drive and to the Library in Windows Media Player. This enables you to listen to an album using your computer's speakers without having to put the CD into your optical drive each time. The process of adding tracks from a CD to your computer and Windows Media Player is called *ripping*.

Windows Media Player functions in two modes: Now Playing and Library. The mode you see when you open Windows Media Player depends on the mode in which you last used Windows Media Player.

Copy Music CD Tracks to Your Computer

① Insert a CD into your computer's optical drive.

Note: *If the AutoPlay window appears, click* ▨.

② Click here to open Windows Media Player.

Note: *Perform Step 3 only if Windows Media Player opens in Now Playing mode and you see the Go to Library button. Otherwise, skip to Step 4.*

③ Click **Go to Library**.

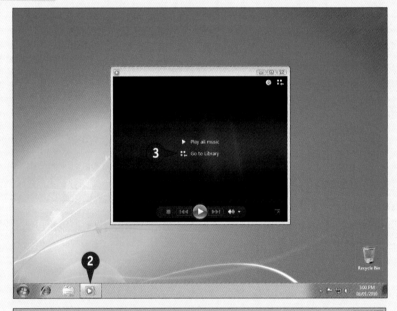

The Library mode appears.

④ Click the optical drive containing the music CD.

Windows Media Player displays a list of the CD's tracks.

5 Click any CD tracks that you do not want to copy (☑ changes to ☐).

6 Click **Rip CD**.

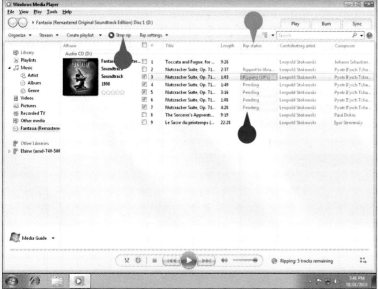

Windows Media Player begins copying the tracks.

● The Rip Status column displays the progress.

● If you want to cancel the operation before it is complete, you can click **Stop rip**.

● After each file is copied, the Rip Status column displays a Ripped to Library message.

Note: *The copy is complete when all the tracks you selected display the Ripped to Library status.*

Can I adjust the quality of the copies?
Yes. You do that by changing the audio quality, which is measured in kilobits per second (Kbps): the higher the value, the higher the quality, but the more disk space each track takes up. Before Step **6**, click **Rip settings**. From the menu that appears, click **Audio Quality**. From the menu that appears, click the value you want.

| 32 Kbps (Smallest size) |
| 48 Kbps |
| ✓ 64 Kbps (Default) |
| 96 Kbps |
| 128 Kbps |
| 160 Kbps |
| 192 Kbps (Best quality) |

Play Music Using Your Computer

You can use Windows Media Player to play music through your computer. Windows Media Player is a free utility that comes with Windows 7. You can play music with or without a music CD; to play music without using the music CD, you must first rip the CD tracks to your computer. See "Copy Music CD Tracks to Your Computer" for details.

Windows Media Player helps you manage and navigate your media library and play back and record audio files and music CDs. Windows Media Player also displays pictures and plays videos, but this section focuses on using Windows Media Player to play music.

Play Music Using Your Computer

Play a CD

1 Insert a music CD in your computer's optical drive.

2 If the AutoPlay window appears, click **Play audio CD**.

Windows Media Player appears, playing the CD in Now Playing mode.

● On commercial CDs, the album cover appears here.

● You can move ⌖ into the Windows Media Player window to view playback controls.

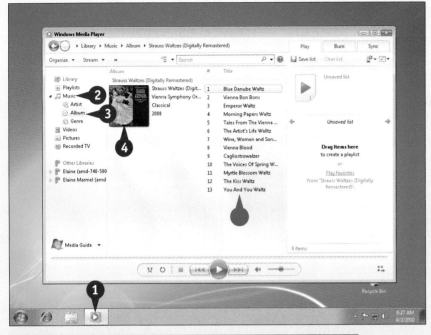

Play Tracks on Your Hard Drive

1. Open Windows Media Player.

   Note: See "Copy Music CD Tracks to Your Computer" to open Windows Media Player.

2. Double-click **Music**.

3. Click **Album**.

4. Double-click the album you want to play.

● The album's tracks appear here.

5. Select the tracks you want to play.

   Note: You can press and hold **Ctrl** *as you click to select multiple individual tracks.*

6. Click and drag the tracks to the Play list.

● The tracks appear in the Play list and Windows Media Player begins playing the tracks.

● The track currently playing appears blue with a small carat beside it.

● You can click **Switch to Now Playing** (⊞) to display only the album art and playback controls.

Simplify It

Is there another way to just play a single track that I have ripped to my computer?
Yes. Open Windows Explorer and navigate to the folder containing the track you want to play — typically, a folder inside the My Music folder — and double-click the track you want to play.

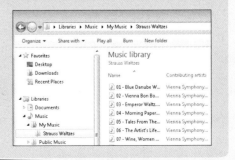

Create a Music CD

You can create a CD of music tracks stored on your computer. When you copy music tracks to a CD, you *burn* them to the CD. Burning a music CD enables you to make a backup of music you buy and download from the Internet. It also enables you to create customized CDs that contain tracks from different albums.

You can use Windows Media Player to burn tracks to a music CD. The process involves selecting the songs you want to burn to the CD; as you burn your CD, Windows Media Player shows you the progress.

Create a Music CD

① Open Windows Media Player.

Note: *See "Copy Music CD Tracks to Your Computer" to open Windows Media Player.*

② Insert a blank CD into your computer's optical drive.

③ In Library mode, click the **Burn** tab.

● The amount of available recording time on the CD appears here.

④ Double-click **Music**.

⑤ Click **Album**.

⑥ Double-click the album containing the tracks you want to burn to a CD.

● The album's tracks appear here.

⑦ Select the tracks you want to burn.

Note: *You can press and hold* Ctrl *as you click to select multiple individual tracks.*

⑧ Click and drag the tracks to the Burn list.

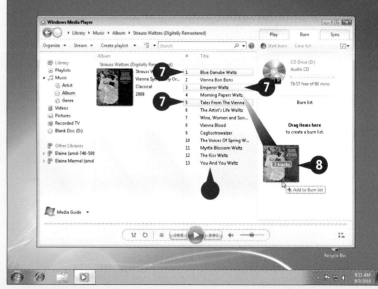

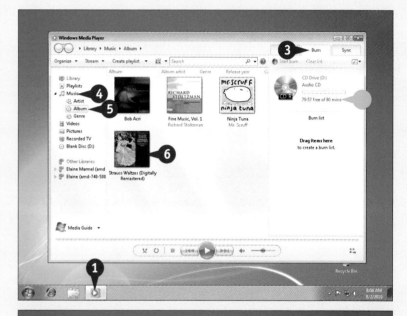

172

● The tracks appear in the Burn list.

● Windows Media Player updates the approximate amount of available space on the CD.

9 Click **Start burn**.

Windows Media Player converts the files to CD tracks and copies them to the CD.

● The progress of the burn operation appears here.

When the burn finishes, Windows Media Player ejects the disc.

Simplify It

How do I burn tracks from different albums onto the same CD?
Select tracks from different albums to burn onto one CD by repeating Steps **5** to **8** before you perform Step **9**.

Do I have to burn the songs in the order they appear in the Burn list?
No, you can reorder the Burn list in several ways, but one method gives you the most control over the order: Place all the tracks you want to burn in the Burn list. Then, drag them up and down in the Burn list until they appear in the order you want.

Discover Gaming

You can play video games on your TV or your PC. Some games do not require any special hardware, and you play these games primarily on your PC using your keyboard and your mouse.

Other games are more complex and are best played by connecting a special device called a *gaming console* to your TV. You typically purchase or rent games designed to work with your console. Examples of gaming consoles include the Microsoft Xbox 360, the Sony PlayStation 3, and the Nintendo Wii.

Windows Games

Windows 7 comes with a series of games you can play using just your keyboard and mouse. These games are installed by default in Windows 7 Home Premium edition and are available but not installed by default in Windows 7 Professional edition and above. See the section "Windows 7 Games" for details. You play some of these games, such as Internet Backgammon, online against other players. You play other games, such as Chess Titans, against the computer. Still other games are single player games, such as Minesweeper.

Gaming Console and Gamepad

A *gaming console* is a specialized computer optimized for playing video games. The gaming console comes without a monitor; for display, the gaming console typically uses your TV or a computer monitor. Besides playing games, you can play DVD movies or music CDs on many gaming consoles.

Most gaming consoles also come with a *gamepad*, which is a specialized, handheld input device that makes the gaming console more powerful and easier to use.

Connect to a TV

Most gaming consoles do not come with a video screen. Instead, you connect the console to your TV. Each gaming console comes with a cable that connects to the back of the console. The other end of the cable has jacks that connect to the ports of the same color on the back of your TV; typically these ports are either yellow, white, and red, or green, blue, and red.

Games

A *video game* is a software program designed to entertain, educate, or challenge you. Most games fall into one of the following categories: action, adventure, arcade, role-playing, simulation, sports, or strategy. PC games require no special equipment; if you plan to play games using a gaming console, be sure to buy or rent games designed to work with your console.

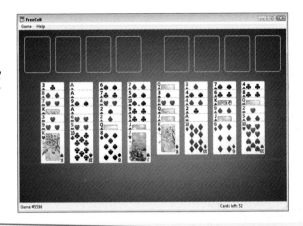

Game Ratings

Most games come with ratings that tell you who should play the game. The Entertainment Software Rating Board (ESRB; see www.esrb.org) has ratings such as T for Teen, AO for Adults Only, and E for Everyone. The ESRB ratings also include content descriptors such as Mature Humor and Strong Language.

ESRB Game Ratings

Search Results

Your search returned 19359 Game Ratings.

Title	Publisher	Rating
Arcade Essentials	Nordcurrent	Everyone
This is a collection of arcade-style games in space-themed game boards. Mini-games inc before a platform reaches the bottom of the		
NHL 2K11	2K Games	Everyone 10+

Online Gaming

You can play both PC games and gaming console games with other users by connecting your hardware to the Internet and then signing up with an online site that enables you to play games over the Internet. Example sites include Xbox Live (www.xbox.com/live), PlayStation 3 Network (us.playstation.com/psn), Yahoo! Games (games.yahoo.com), and the Multiplayer Online Games Directory (www.mpogd.com).

Windows 7 Games

Windows 7 comes with several games, including both games you can play against the computer and games you can play with others over the Internet. The games are installed by default in Windows 7 Home Premium edition, but not in Windows 7 Professional edition and above. However, the games are available in all editions of Windows 7; you simply have to install them.

Once you install games, they appear in a folder of their own on the Start menu. Most Windows 7 games display tips when you open the window and as you play. You also can use the Help menu to find more information about a game.

Install Games

1 Click the **Start** button (⊞).

2 Click **Control Panel**.

The Control Panel window appears.

3 Click **Programs**.

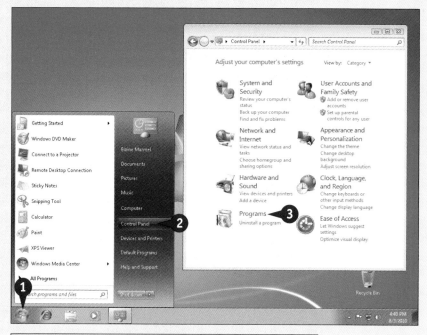

The Programs window appears.

4 Click **Turn Windows features on or off**.

The Windows Features dialog box appears.

5 Click **Games** (☐ changes to ☑).

6 Click **OK**.

Windows 7 installs games.

7 Click ⊠ to close the Control Panel window.

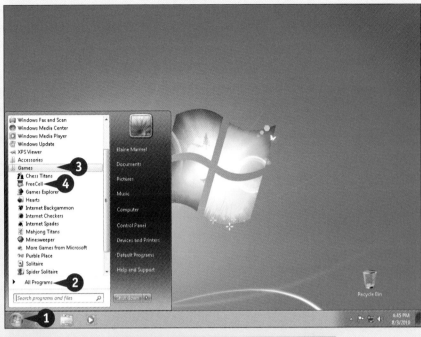

Play a Game

1 Click the **Start** button (🔲).

2 Click **All Programs**.

3 Click **Games**.

4 Click a game.

The game window appears.

What is the Games Explorer choice in the Games folder?
When you click **Games Explorer**, Windows Explorer opens to a window
that displays the games and game providers installed on your computer.
When you click a game or game provider, you see more information
about it in the right-hand pane; you can click the tabs in the middle of the
right-hand pane to view the game rating, performance on your computer,
and game statistics — games played, games won, streaks, and so on.

Chapter 9

Working with Portable Computers and Devices

Portable computers are not limited to notebook PCs; smartphones and music devices are actually portable computers. This chapter presents a broad overview of portable computers and shows you how to synchronize information from a BlackBerry smartphone and an iPod with your desktop computer.

Understand the Advantages of a Portable Computer

The term *portable computer* applies to a wide variety of devices. You are probably familiar with notebook computers (also called *laptops*), but you might not realize that cell phones are also portable computers. Most portable computers are as powerful as a desktop computer, but they are also lightweight and small enough to take with you when you leave your office or home. Because they are battery-powered, you do not need an electrical connection to run them. And, if necessary, you can connect a portable device to your desktop computer.

Lightweight

Portable computers are designed to be light enough to take with you wherever you go. A notebook generally weighs around 5 or 6 pounds, and a netbook, the notebook computer's *lightweight* cousin, generally weighs around 2 pounds. Smartphones and portable music devices like the iPod generally weigh only a few ounces.

Powerful

Depending on the configuration, notebook computers can be just as powerful as desktop systems. Netbooks have limitations but can do many of the things a desktop system can do, such as run word-processing and spreadsheet software, access the Internet, and collect e-mail. Smartphones are getting smarter every day; they can help you manage your calendar, contacts, and "to do" list, and you can run applications on them and access the Internet and e-mail with them.

Connection-Free

Notebook and netbook computers and smartphones all come with a keyboard, mouse, and screen packaged into a single, self-contained unit. This makes portable computers easy to set up and use because, for basic operations, you do not need to connect anything to the device.

Battery Operation

Desktop systems require an AC outlet. Portable devices, on the other hand, can run off their internal batteries if AC power is not available. Internal batteries enable you to use a portable computer almost anywhere, including a coffee shop, taxi, airplane, and even a park.

Security and Portable Devices

The advantage of portability is also a disadvantage: Portable devices can be lost or stolen. Many notebook computers come with fingerprint readers so that only their owners can use them. Many notebook computer users also encrypt the notebook's hard drive to make retrieving information difficult for a thief. Smartphones usually include some technique that enables you to lock them and require a password to unlock them.

Connect to Desktop PC

You can connect notebooks and netbooks to your desktop computer using a *docking station*, which is a peripheral device you connect to your desktop. Then, using a USB cable, you connect your notebook to the docking station. Once connected, you can use your desktop PC's keyboard and monitor to operate your notebook. You also can connect handheld devices such as a smartphone or a music player to your desktop computer using a USB cable; once connected, you can synchronize information on these devices with information on your desktop PC.

Discover Portable Devices

A portable device is a small computer that varies in size. The biggest are no bigger than a business briefcase, and the smallest fit comfortably in your hand or in a jacket pocket. Some portable devices can do the work of desktop computers, whereas other portable devices supplement the desktop computer by providing a mobile way to store and retrieve your schedule and to check e-mail while out of the office.

Notebooks

Notebook computers, if properly configured with memory and hard disk space, can generally do almost everything a desktop computer can do. Notebook computers typically weigh around 5 or 6 pounds and come with network cards and optical drives, so you can easily connect to the Internet or a network of computers, and you can easily install software or listen to music on CDs.

Netbooks

A *netbook* is a smaller notebook computer, weighing around 2 pounds. To reduce their weight, netbooks come with network cards but without optical drives, and netbook screens are smaller than notebook screens. Netbooks also contain less memory and smaller hard drives than notebooks. You can use netbooks to produce small word-processing documents or spreadsheets and to connect to the Internet, surf the Web, and collect, read, and answer e-mail.

Smartphones

A smartphone is a cell phone that also doubles as a personal digital organizer, helping you manage your calendar, tasks, and contacts. Smartphones like the BlackBerry from Research In Motion also can run small applications, play music, store images, take photos and videos, and, using a wireless connection, connect to the Internet, and send and receive e-mail.

Reading Devices

In the strictest sense, reading devices like the Kindle from Amazon or the NOOK from Barnes and Noble are not computers because they do not accept traditional input. But you can buy and wirelessly download electronic books from the Internet and read them on these devices, enabling you to carry as many books as you want wherever you go. You also can surf the Internet and load and read word-processing and spreadsheet documents using these devices.

Music Players

The iPod has become the portable music player of choice. You can download music to an iPod and then listen to the music whenever and wherever you want. Many people like to listen to music while they exercise or while on airplanes using the headphones that come with the iPod.

Operating Systems

Some portable devices, like notebooks and netbooks, use the Windows 7 operating system; netbooks are the only computers on which you find Windows 7 Starter edition. Smartphones and reading devices use their own special operating systems, designed to work with their limited memory and smaller screen.

Synchronize with a PC

If you connect your smartphone or music player to your desktop computer using a USB cable, you can then use special software that also comes with the device to synchronize the data on the desktop with the data on the portable device. For example, you could update your smartphone schedule with new appointments that you have added while working on your desktop.

Synchronize Using a BlackBerry Smartphone

The BlackBerry smartphone is among the most popular of the smartphones; it not only acts as a cell phone, but it connects to the Internet, collects e-mail, and manages personal information such as your calendar, your "to do" list, your address book, and your notes to yourself.

Along with collecting e-mail, Microsoft Outlook also supports personal information functions. Using the BlackBerry Desktop Manager software, you can synchronize personal information and e-mail between Outlook and your BlackBerry. This section shows you how to synchronize and assumes you have set up synchronization between Outlook and the BlackBerry Desktop Manager.

Synchronize Using a BlackBerry Smartphone

1 Connect the cable that came with your BlackBerry to the BlackBerry and to a USB port on your computer.

2 Click the **Start** button (🔵).

3 Click **All Programs**.

4 Click **BlackBerry**.

5 Click **BlackBerry Desktop Software**.

The BlackBerry Desktop Manager loads, initializes, checks for application updates, and then presents its interface.

6 Click **Sync All**.

● You can click **Organizer** to set up synchronization options between your BlackBerry device and Outlook.

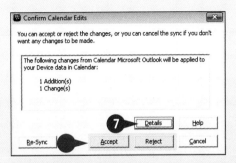

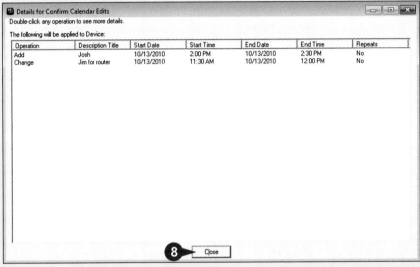

A progress bar appears and, if differences exist between Outlook and your BlackBerry, a dialog box appears.

● You can click **Accept** to allow updating for all changes or **Reject** to avoid updating for all changes.

➐ To view the changes, click **Details**.

A window appears, displaying the differences between the BlackBerry device and Outlook. When resolving a conflict, you can choose the information to use.

➑ Review the changes and click **Close**.

The window that summarized the changes reappears.

➒ Click **Accept** to allow updating for all changes or **Reject** to avoid updating for all changes.

The synchronization process completes and, if you allowed changes, the information in your BlackBerry and Outlook matches.

How do I set up synchronization between Outlook and the BlackBerry Desktop Manager?
Setting up synchronization is a one-time operation. Click **Organizer** on the left side of the BlackBerry Desktop Manager. Then, click the **Configure Settings** button. A screen appears that you can use to establish Outlook as the software with which you want to synchronize the BlackBerry device. A wizard walks you through the configuration process.

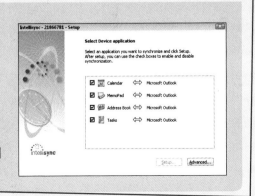

Synchronize Using an iPod

Using your iPod and iTunes, you can synchronize all media that your iPod supports with media on your computer. Using the iTunes store, which is part of iTunes, you can buy media online from your computer or wirelessly using your iPod and synchronize it.

iTunes is free, and you download it from the Internet. When you connect an iPod to your

computer, iTunes automatically loads and synchronizes music on your computer to your iPod and media you buy wirelessly from your iPod to your computer. This section focuses on what happens the first time you connect an iPod to your computer. It assumes you have downloaded and installed iTunes.

Synchronize Using an iPod

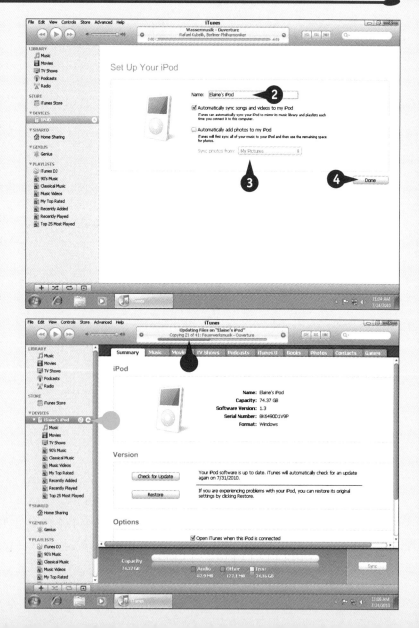

1 Connect the cable that came with your iPod to the iPod and to a USB port on your computer.

iTunes loads.

Note: *If you opted to do so during installation, iTunes imports music from your computer.*

iTunes prompts you to set up the connected device.

2 Click here and type a name for the connected device.

3 Click here to select the types of media you want to synchronize to your iPod (▢ changes to ☑).

4 Click **Done**.

● The name you assigned to your iPod appears here.

iTunes begins synchronizing the media you specified from your computer to your iPod.

● You can monitor the progress here.

● Use this box to determine whether synchronization has completed.

⑤ Once synchronization completes, click media types under Library.

● The media iTunes imported from your computer appears here.

● You can click these buttons to view the media in a list, as album covers (as shown here), or a combination of both.

⑥ Click a media category under your iPod device.

● The items transferred to your iPod appear in list form.

● If you do not see media categories under your device, click the triangle immediately to the left of your device's name.

How do I get iTunes to load music stored on my computer?

The first time you open iTunes a wizard appears and offers to add music already on your computer to iTunes. If you subsequently add music to your computer using some method other than iTunes, you can add that music to iTunes. Click **File** and then click **Add Folder to Library**. Click the folder and click **Select Folder**.

Chapter 10

Surfing the World Wide Web

The Internet contains a vast wealth of information, both educational and entertaining. To take advantage of the rich diversity of the Internet, you need to understand what the Internet is about and how you can connect to it so that you can use Internet Explorer or another browser to navigate the Web sites on the World Wide Web.

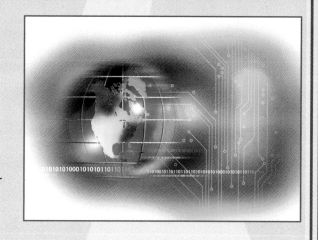

Introduction to the Internet

The Internet is a vast collection of connected networks that span the world. You can think of the Internet as a network of networks. Using the Internet, you can read the latest news, do research, shop, communicate with others, listen to music, play games, watch TV and movies, and access a wide variety of information.

The Internet began in the late 1960s as a project sponsored by the United States Defense Department. Over time, the Internet expanded to include other government agencies, universities, research labs, businesses, and individuals.

Worldwide Network

The Internet is a worldwide network. Similar to a local area network, where you can work with shared resources on other computers, you can use an Internet *browser* to view and share information on other computers around the world. The Internet's backbone is a collection of connected telephone lines, fiber-optic cables, and satellites that span the world. Data travels along this backbone.

Internet Service Provider

An *Internet service provider* (ISP) is a company that has direct access to the Internet backbone. The ISP sets up a network of servers that connect to the Internet, and you use a modem to access the ISP's network and connect to the Internet.

Bandwidth

The more bandwidth you have, the faster the response while working on the Internet. Digital subscriber line (DSL) telephone services, television cable hookups, and satellite dishes all provide high bandwidth connections — called *broadband connections* — to the Internet. You use a high-speed modem to make a broadband connection to the Internet.

The World Wide Web

The World Wide Web is an interlinked collection of data. It is divided into separate pages, where each page has information on a specific topic. Most pages have at least one link that you can click to take you to a related page. There are billions of Web pages that cover millions of topics.

E-Mail

You can use electronic mail, or simply e-mail, to send and receive messages. Unlike postal mail messages, e-mail messages are delivered anywhere in the world within minutes, and you do not pay an extra charge to send them. For more information about e-mail, see Chapter 11.

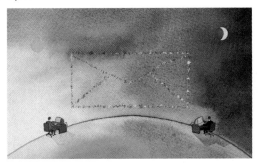

Instant Messaging

You can use instant messaging to send and receive messages. These messages are like e-mail but exchanged instantly, so they more closely resemble a telephone conversation.

Media

You can use the Internet to play songs and listen to radio stations. You can also run animations, view movie trailers, watch television and videos, and access many other types of media. For more information about multimedia, see Chapter 8.

Explore Internet Connections

To connect to the Internet, you need equipment and services. For equipment, your computer must contain a network interface adaptor, and you need a broadband modem and possibly a router. You should determine the type of connection you want to make to the Internet and then select an Internet service provider who can offer you the type of connection you want. You must open an account with the Internet Service provider, who then provides you with the information you need to log on to the Internet.

Internet Service Provider

You cannot access the Internet directly. Instead, you must sign up for an account with an Internet service provider (ISP). Your ISP provides you with a username and password information and might, in some cases, come to your home and set up your Internet connection for you. The ISP you choose determines the type of broadband connection you make to the Internet.

Network Card

Your computer must contain a network interface adaptor to connect to the Internet. Remember, the Internet is a huge network. To connect to any network, you need a network card in your computer. If you intend to connect wirelessly, make sure you purchase a network card specifically designed to make a wireless connection.

Connection Types

Digital subscriber line (DSL) telephone services, television cable hookups, and satellite dishes all provide broadband connections to the Internet. The DSL connection resembles a telephone line, whereas the cable and satellite connections use television cable. These connections are "always on" connections; turning on your computer connects you to the Internet.

Modem

Regardless of the connection type, you use a high-speed modem to make a broadband connection to the Internet. Some ISPs supply modems; if yours does not, you might be able to buy a modem from your ISP, or you can ask them to recommend a model and then shop for it on your own.

Router

Although a router is not a necessity, having one is advisable because it contains a firewall that helps make your computer invisible while connected to the Internet. Being invisible while using the Internet helps to protect your privacy and keep your computer safe from intruders.

Set Up Your Internet Equipment

Before you start your computer for the first time or for the first time after installing a network card, establish your physical connection. If you use only a modem, connect a cable directly from the modem to your computer's network card. If you opt to use a router, connect a cable from your computer's network card to the router. Then, connect a cable from the modem to the Internet port on the router (it might be called WAN or Uplink).

Manually Establish an Internet Connection

Once you have inserted a network card in your computer, signed up for an Internet access account with an Internet service provider (ISP), attached your modem either directly to your computer or to a router that is also connected to your computer, you are ready to connect to the Internet.

In most cases, Windows 7 establishes your Internet connection for you automatically the first time you turn on your computer after installing a network card. This section provides you with steps in the event that you need to set up the connection manually.

Manually Establish an Internet Connection

1 Click the **Start** button (🟦).

2 Click **Control Panel**.

The Control Panel window appears.

3 Click **View network status and tasks**.

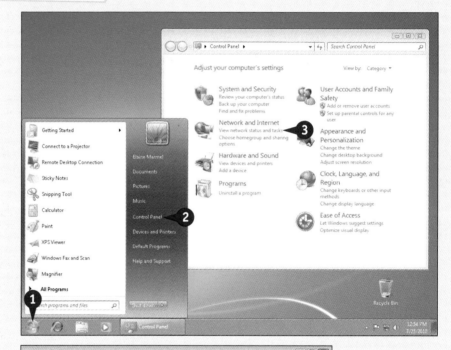

The Network and Sharing Center window appears.

4 Click **Set up a new connection or network**.

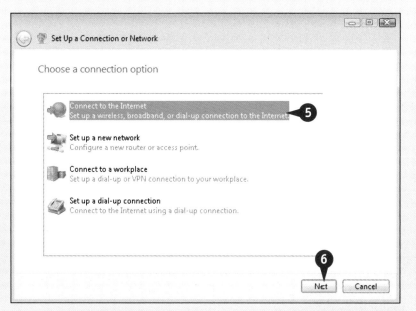

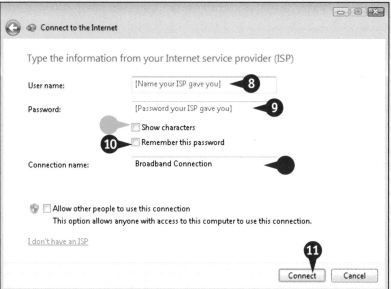

The Set Up a Connection or Network wizard starts.

⑤ Click **Connect to the Internet**.

⑥ Click **Next**.

The How Do You Want to Connect? window appears.

⑦ Click **Broadband (PPPoE)**.

The Type the Information from Your Internet Service Provider (ISP) window appears.

⑧ Type the username you received from your ISP here.

⑨ Type the password you received from your ISP here.

● You can click here to display the characters of your password instead of dots (☐ changes to ☑).

⑩ Click here to avoid having to provide your password each time you log on to the Internet (☐ changes to ☑).

● You can type a new name for the connection here.

⑪ Click **Connect**.

The home page of your default browser appears. See "World Wide Web Basics" for more information.

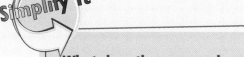

What does the screen where I select a connection look like?
By default, Windows 7 displays only those connection options your computer can use.

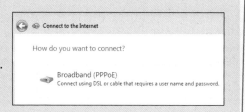

195

Guard Against Internet Intruders

An Internet intruder is a person who attempts to gain access to your computer or network through your Internet connection. The intruder's goal is to examine your confidential data, destroy files, install a virus, or steal your passwords or your identity. The intruder may want to commandeer your computer and use it to attack Web sites; hijacked computers are called *zombies*.

You can set up your computer or network to prevent such intrusions. Make sure that you enable a firewall and use antivirus and anti-spyware protection.

Antivirus and Anti-Spyware Software

Antivirus and anti-spyware software programs protect your computer from malware. Unfortunately, the Internet is a great place to pick up infections from viruses and spyware, so, locking down your computer against them is essential. Windows 7 comes with a spyware program called Windows Defender. Microsoft Security Essentials and AVG are two popular, free programs that guard against both viruses and spyware.

Firewall

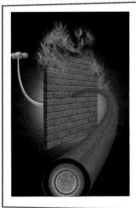

A *firewall* is a software program, device, or computer that restricts the type of data that can pass from the Internet to a person's computer or network by blocking the virtual ports that outsiders can use to view and access the computer. In this way, the firewall prevents unauthorized users from gaining access to the computer or network.

Windows 7 Firewall

Windows 7 comes with a built-in firewall program. Although not the most powerful firewall program available, it is adequate when combined with other tools, such as a hardware firewall, antivirus protection, and anti-spyware protection.

Help protect your computer with Windows Firewall

Windows Firewall can help prevent hackers or malicious software from gaining access to your computer through the Internet or a network.

How does a firewall help protect my computer?

What are network locations?

Home or work (private) networks   Connected

Networks at home or work where you know and trust the people and devices on the network

Windows Firewall state: On

Hardware Firewall

A *hardware firewall* is a device that contains a firewall to protect a computer or a network from intrusion — the most common hardware firewall is found in a router. Therefore, using a router provides another secure layer of protection while working on the Internet. Though not a requirement for using the Internet, it is advisable to use a router in your computer configuration.

Third-Party Firewalls

You can install a firewall from a third-party software vendor to further lock down your computer. Most of these programs offer more features than the firewall included in Windows 7. However, many people find the pop-up messages from a firewall confusing and tend to simply allow access when they should deny it, defeating the purpose of the firewall. Using the Windows 7 firewall with a router should provide you with sufficient protection.

Test Your Firewall

To ensure that your firewall is working correctly, there are Internet sites that can test it for you. Try Gibson Research Corporation's ShieldsUP! (www.grc.com) or HackerWhacker (www.hackerwhacker.com).

World Wide Web Basics

The World Wide Web, or simply the Web, is a massive storehouse of information that resides on computers, called *Web servers*, located all over the world. These Web servers are connected by optical fiber or satellite links so that they can share information. The Web servers are operated by Internet service providers (ISPs), who sell access to individuals. When you use a username and password that an ISP provides to you to log onto the Internet, you actually connect to the ISP's Web servers, which route you to the Internet.

To work effectively on the Internet, you need to know a few terms.

Web Page

World Wide Web information is presented on Web pages that you view using a Web browser program, such as Internet Explorer. Each Web page can combine text with images, sounds, music, and even videos to present information on a particular subject. The Web consists of billions of pages covering almost every imaginable topic.

Web Site

A Web site is a collection of Web pages associated with a particular person, business, government, school, or organization. Some Web sites deal with only a single topic, but most sites contain pages on a variety of topics.

Web Server

Web sites are stored on *Web servers*, which are special computers connected around the world to make Web pages available for people to browse. A Web server is usually a powerful computer capable of handling thousands of site visitors at a time. The largest Web sites are run by *server farms*, which are networks that may contain dozens or even hundreds of servers.

Web Browser

A *Web browser* is a software program designed to download and display Web pages. Windows 7 ships with the Web browser Internet Explorer 8, but you can download other Web browsers, such as Mozilla Firefox and Google Chrome.

Links

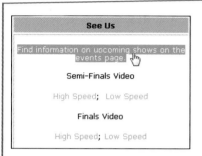

A *link* is an interactive connection to another location on the Web. A link takes you to another location on the current page, to another page on the same site, or to a page on another Web site. Links can appear as text or images. A text link is often underlined or uses a different color from the regular text on the page. It also can appear in reverse video when you position your mouse over it, and typically, the mouse pointer changes to a hand when positioned over a link. When you click a link, your Web browser loads the page associated with the link.

Web Address

Every Web site and Web page has its own Web address that uniquely identifies the page. This address is the *Uniform Resource Locator*, or *URL* (pronounced yoo-ar-ell). If you know the address of a page, you can type that address into your Web browser to view the page.

The URL of a Web site or page is composed of three basic parts: the transfer method (usually http, which stands for HyperText Transfer Protocol), the Web site domain name, which is the directory where the Web page is located on the Web server, and the Web page filename.

The Web site domain name most often uses the .com (business) suffix, but other common suffixes include .gov (government), .org (nonprofit organization), and country domains such as .ca (Canada) and .uk (United Kingdom).

Learn About
Web Browsers

You can easily surf the Web if you know your way around your Web browser. A Web browser is a software program. Each software program has a purpose. Word-processing software helps you handle text. Spreadsheet software helps you handle numbers. A Web browser is the type of program you use to view Web pages.

Windows 7 comes with a Web browser called Internet Explorer, but, as with other software programs, you are not limited to using Internet Explorer; you have choices. And, most Web browsers work in similar ways.

Popular Web Browsers

Internet Explorer

Internet Explorer is the browser that comes with Windows 7 and most other versions of Windows. Internet Explorer is the most widely used Web browser. You can find updates and more information at www.microsoft.com/windows/ie/.

Firefox

Firefox is the free browser offered by the Mozilla Foundation. It is *open-source* software, which means that Firefox was created through a collaborative effort by a community of programmers. Firefox is available for Windows and OS X at www.mozilla.org/products/firefox/.

Chrome

Although Google made its start as a search engine, it has expanded its offerings dramatically. Among those offerings is Chrome, Google's browser, available for free download from www.google.com/chrome.

Web Browser Features

Address Bar

This text box shows the address of the displayed Web page. You can also use the address bar to type the address of a Web page that you want to visit.

Navigation Buttons

Each Web browser has navigation buttons that enable you to move back and forth through recently visited pages. For example, with Internet Explorer, you can click **Back** (⬅) to move to the previous page that you visited and click **Forward** (➡) to move to the next page that you visited.

Search Box

You use the Search box to locate pages on the Web.

Favorites Bar

Called the Bookmarks Bar by both Firefox and Chrome, this bar contains buttons that help you navigate to Web sites you visit frequently. You add buttons to this bar using different techniques in each browser.

Browser Tabs

Most of the major Web browsers make *tabbed browsing* available to you, which enables you to open multiple Web sites. The name of each Web page appears in the browser tab. If you click the small space behind the current tab, you open a new placeholder browser tab, and you can type a URL or search the Web. The original browser tab remains open, and you can go back to that page whenever you want by clicking that tab.

Link

On some pages, such as the one shown here, the link text also is underlined and changes color after you click it. When you position the mouse pointer over a link, the mouse pointer changes from ⤢ to ⬆.

Status Bar

This area displays the current status of the Web browser. For example, in Internet Explorer, it displays a green status bar as you wait for a Web page to appear, and Done when the page is fully loaded. When you position the mouse pointer over a link, the status bar displays the address of the page associated with the link.

Search the Web

If you need information on a specific topic, you can use free Web sites called *search engines* to help you quickly search the Web for pages that have the information you require. These search engines index Web pages by content and serve much the same purpose as the card catalog in a public library. You supply search terms, and the search engine displays a list of Web pages that match the search terms.

You can search the Web either by going directly to a search engine site or by using the Search box built into your browser.

Search Engine Sites

Here are the addresses of popular search engines:

Search Engine	URL
Alta Vista	www.altavista.com
Ask	www.ask.com
Bing	www.bing.com
Google	www.google.com
Live Search	www.live.com
Yahoo!	search.yahoo.com

Web Browser Searching

To search the Web from Internet Explorer, click inside the Search box, type a word, phrase, or question that you want to find, and then click 🔎. The Web browser displays a list of links to sites that match your search text.

Search engines index the Web by using special programs. These worker ants — called *Web crawlers* or *Web bots* — catalog each Web page and its content. Many search engines also enable individuals to submit information about their Web pages. Google, the largest search engine, indexes several billion Web pages.

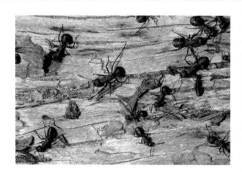

Search Techniques

The Web is so large that simple, one-word searches often return tens of thousands of *hits*, or matching sites. To improve your searching and reduce the number of pages a search engine returns, type multiple search terms that define what you are looking for. To search for a phrase, enclose the words in quotation marks.

Search Types

By default, search engines return links to those Web pages that match your search criteria. However, the Web is about more than just text. It also contains images, music and audio files, video files, and news. Most of the larger search engines enable you to search for these different types of content. Often you can simply add the media type to your search string.

hard drive video

About 117,000,000 results (0.25 seconds)

Hard Drive Video On Sale
BHPhoto**Video**.com   Save On **Video** "**Hard Drive**" Low Pric
BHPhoto**Video**.com is rated ☆☆☆☆☆ on Google Products (159

Videos for **hard drive video**

Inside of **Hard Drive**
2 min - Oct 1, 2006
Uploaded by joshuamarius
www.youtube.com

Search Strategies

Many search engines have advanced search capabilities that enable you to type several terms and find sites that match at least one of the terms or eliminate sites that match terms you specify. To use these advanced capabilities, navigate to the search engine's Web site and look for a link to advanced searching ( ).

Read News on the Web

The Web is home to many sites that enable you to read the latest news. Many print sources have Web sites, and you can read all kinds of news electronically — newspapers, magazines, and blogs.

Newspapers

Print media such as newspapers and magazines have embraced the Web as a way to augment their traditional business. Some companies have Web sites with up-to-the-minute stories, whereas others use their sites just as archives of previously published stories. Some media sites require that you register to access the articles, but on most sites, the registration is free.

Magazines

A number of Web news sources exist as online magazines, also called *e-zines*. Many of these online publications offer a wide variety of content and excellent writing. To find e-zines that might interest you, search the Web using the search term "e-zines." The search results contain several directories that list e-zines by category.

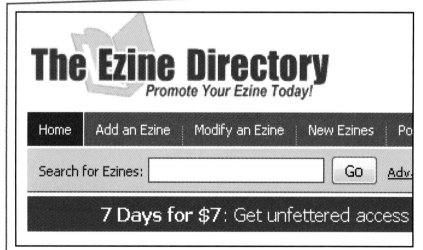

Blogs

A *blog* — or *Web log* — is a Web page consisting of frequently updated, reverse-chronological entries made by the blogger. Some blogs are mere diaries or lists of interesting links, but many have a news focus, particularly news on politics, such as www.instapundit.com, and technology, such as www.techcrunch.com.

News Portal

A *news portal* is a Web site that gathers news from hundreds or even thousands of online sources. You can then search the news, browse headlines, and view news by subject. Two popular news portals are NewsIsFree (www. newsisfree.com) and NewsNow (www.newsnow. co.uk). The major search engines also maintain news portals, such as Google News (news. google.com).

Syndication

Instead of surfing to a Web media site or news portal, you can have articles and news headlines sent to you. Many news sites use syndication, which enables a special program called an *aggregator* — also called an *RSS reader* (RSS is short for Real Simple Syndication) — to display the syndicated content. You see a symbol like this one on such sites.

Research Using the Web

You can use the Web's vast resources to research just about any topic you can imagine. The Web has information that can help you with a school project, your family history, or a presentation at work. You can search for the data that you need, or go to specific research sites.

Be aware that not all of the information on the Web is factual or useful. Sites often have inaccurate or deliberately misleading data. In general, stick to large, reputable sites and be sure to locate information you think is factual on more than one site.

Reference Materials

Sites such as Encarta (encarta.msn.com) and Britannica (www.britannica.com) offer multiple online research tools, including encyclopedias, dictionaries, and atlases. The Web is also home to thousands of sites that offer almanacs, maps, and thesauruses.

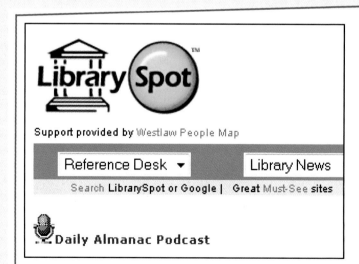

Libraries and Museums

Many public and private libraries maintain Web sites that enable you to search their catalogs, access their digital archives, and order books; you can find many of these libraries using LibrarySpot (www.libraryspot. com). Many museums are also online, offering articles and interactive exhibits.

Government Resources

Federal, state, and municipal government Web sites contain a wealth of information on a wide variety of topics. Depending on the level of government, you can use these sites to research trends, statistics, regulations, laws and bylaws, patents, and trademarks. Most government sites, like www.irs.gov and www.ssa.gov, also offer articles, papers, essays, and learning kits.

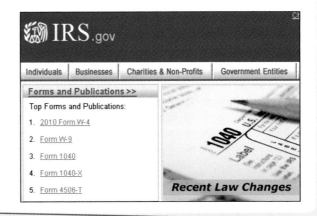

People and Genealogy

If you are trying to find a person, the Web has hundreds of sites that enable you to search for phone numbers, postal and e-mail addresses, and old classmates. If you are trying to find your ancestors, the Web also boasts hundreds of genealogy sites. Either you can search directly using online resources such as birth and death records, or you can use dedicated genealogy sites such as Ancestry.com and Genealogy.com.

Ask an Expert

Hundreds of millions of people access the Web, and many of them are experts on one or more topics. You can find many of these experts at "Ask an Expert" sites that enable you to pose questions that experts in the field will answer. Although some sites require a fee, many sites are free, including AllExperts (www.allexperts.com) and Yahoo! Answers (http://answers.yahoo.com).

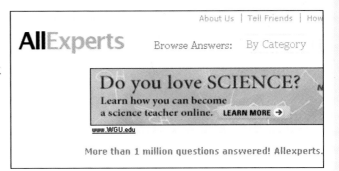

Buy and Sell on the Web

E-commerce is the online buying and selling of goods and services. It is a big part of the Web. You can use Web-based stores to purchase books, theater tickets, and even cars. Many sites also enable you to sell or auction your products or household items.

E-commerce has many advantages. For buying, you have the convenience of shopping at home, easily comparing prices and features, and having goods delivered to your door. For selling, the Web offers low overhead and a potential audience of millions of people.

Buying on the Web

Thousands of Web sites are devoted to online shopping. Some, like Expedia Travel (www.expedia.com), focus on one product or service, whereas others, such as Amazon (www.amazon.com), offer a wide range of goods like traditional department stores. You can also find Web sites for traditional retailers such as Walmart, and many manufacturers enable you to purchase goods directly through their Web sites.

Shopping Cart

When you shop at an e-commerce site, you usually add the items that you want to purchase to a virtual shopping cart — also called a shopping basket — that keeps track of these items and the quantity. Most sites have a View Cart link that enables you to view the contents of your shopping cart. The cart usually has a Proceed to Checkout link that leads you to a page where you provide your address and payment information.

Product Reviews

If you plan to make a purchase, whether it is a computer, a car, or a vacation, you can use the Web to research the product beforehand. There are sites devoted to product reviews by consumers, such as Epinions (www.epinions.com); reviews by companies, such as the J.D. Power Consumer Center (www.jdpower.com); and government resources, such as the Federal Citizen Information Center (www.pueblo.gsa.gov).

Site Security

Purchasing anything on the Web requires that you provide accurate payment data, such as your credit number and expiry date. To ensure that this sensitive data does not fall into the wrong hands, provide this payment data only on a secure site. Your browser may tell you when you are entering a secure site. Otherwise, look for "https" instead of "http" in the site address, and look for a lock icon in the browser window.

Selling on the Web

Virtual Store

Many Web companies offer e-commerce hosting to enable you to set up your own online store. Sites such as Yahoo! Small Business (http://smallbusiness.yahoo.com) offer tools, storage space, and expertise to build and promote your store.

Online Auction

If you make your own products or have household items that you no longer need, you can put them up for sale in an online auction. By far, the most popular general online auction site is eBay (www.ebay.com), but there are also thousands of auction sites devoted to specific items, such as cars or memorabilia. Many auction sellers accept payment through the PayPal service (www.paypal.com), which transfers buyer credit card payments to your bank account.

Socialize on the Web

The Web offers many opportunities to socialize, whether you are looking for a friend or a date, or you just want some good conversation.

The Web is generally a safe place to socialize but, as in the real world, you should observe some common-sense precautions. For example, if you plan to meet new friends face to face, arrange to meet them in public places. Make sure that you supervise all online socializing done by children. Finally, do not give out personal information to strangers, and teach your children not to give out personal information.

Meet Friends

If you are looking to meet new friends, either for the social contact or to expand your network, the Web has sites such as Facebook (www.facebook.com) and MySpace (www.myspace.com) that enable you to meet people with common interests. Two other popular sites are Twitter (www.twitter.com) and LinkedIn (www.linkedin.com), where you can meet new friends through your existing network of friends.

facebook

Facebook helps you connect and share with the people in your life.

eHarmony
Advice
real people. real advice.

5 Dating Rules
Dating isn't eas
experience as a

ALSO: Master the Art of Conversa

Find Dates

There are hundreds of online dating services that cater to all kinds of people looking for all kinds of relationships. Two of the most popular online dating sites are eHarmony (www. eharmony.com) and Match.com. There are also many sites devoted to specific types of people and relationships.

Forums

Many Web sites offer *forums*, which are also called *message boards* or *discussion boards*. These sections within the site enable visitors to post messages that are shown on the site for others to see and reply to. Some forums deal with the site or company, such as the discussion boards on the eBay site, whereas others cover a particular subject, such as the numerous gardening forums hosted by GardenWeb (www.gardenweb.com).

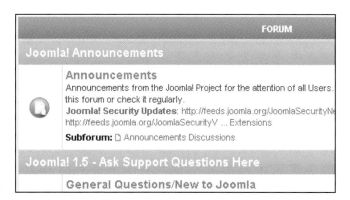

Chat Rooms

A *chat room* is a section on a Web site in which visitors can exchange typed messages in real time. Depending on the popularity of the site, a chat room can contain anywhere from a few people chatting to a few dozen. Many chat services also enable you to switch to a "private" chat room for one-on-one discussions.

Clubs and Pen Pals

In the real world, a pen pal is a person with whom you exchange letters. In the online world, a pen pal is someone with whom you exchange e-mail messages. Because e-mails are typed, online pen pals are sometimes called *keypals*. You can use the Web to find online pen pals, particularly for children. For example, see KeyPals Club International (http://kci.the-protagonist.net/) and ePALS (www.epals.com).

Protect Yourself on the Web

Protecting yourself on the Web means understanding and preventing a number of security and privacy problems. These include problems with spyware, pop-up ads, saved passwords, cookies, and unsecure sites.

Both Internet Explorer and Windows 7 contain some tools you can use to help you maintain your security and privacy. Other browsers also contain similar tools. These tools help you guard against spyware and annoying pop-up ads.

Spyware

Spyware is software that installs on your computer without your knowledge or consent. These programs surreptitiously gather data from your computer, steal your passwords, display advertisements, and hijack your Web browser to cripple your ability to view Web pages of your choice. To eliminate these programs from your computer and prevent spyware from installing on your computer, Windows 7 includes Windows Defender, which is turned on by default.

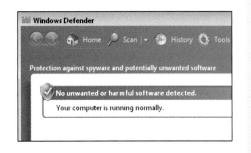

Pop-Up Ads

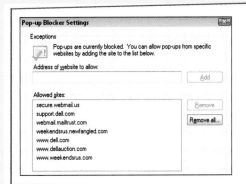

A *pop-up ad* is an advertisement that interrupts your Web browsing by appearing in a separate browser window on top of your current window. Pop-ups are annoying, but also dangerous because clicking items in the pop-up window can cause spyware to install on your computer. Use a pop-up blocker such as the ones built into Internet Explorer and Firefox.

Saved Passwords

When you submit a form that includes a site password, Internet Explorer displays a prompt that offers to remember the password. If you click **Yes** and then access the site at a later date, Internet Explorer bypasses the login page and takes you directly to the site. Unfortunately, a saved password means that anyone else who uses your computer can access the site. Therefore, you may want to click **No** when Internet Explorer asks to remember the password.

Cookies

A *cookie* is a small text file that a Web site stores on your computer to keep track of things such as preferences and shopping cart items. Cookies can also store site usernames and passwords, as well as your credit card data; if possible, tell the site not to save this data. Alternatively, use a cookie manager program such as Cookie Monster (www.ampsoft.net/utilities/CookieMonster.php) or Cookie Pal (www.kburra.com).

Unsecure Sites

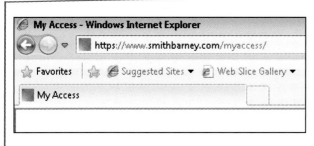

Secure Site Indicators

Information that you send over the Web — such as when you fill out and send a form — is usually sent in plain text that anyone can read. A secure site is one that sends your data in an encrypted format that is impossible to read. Before you send sensitive data such as your credit card number, be sure that the site is secure. In the browser address bar, look for "https" and a lock icon (🔒).

Protected Mode

Internet Explorer's protected mode feature is designed to hamper malicious software from installing itself on your computer without hampering your Web browsing style. With protected mode enabled, Internet Explorer warns you when Web pages try to run or install software. The status bar displays information about the status of protected mode (●).

Got IE8 yet? You can upgrade

⟩HD quiz

⟩nd deals

⟩fter prison

⟩Phone

POPULAR SEARCHES

Fam

From

🌐 Internet | Protected Mode: On

Protect Your Children on the Web

To protect your children on the Web, you need to understand the dangers that await them and learn ways to avoid those dangers. Good browsers give you options to restrict the content that can be shown, and using these controls is a good way to start protecting your children. But it is only a start; as a parent, you need to be involved when your children are browsing the Internet.

Children can very easily come upon inappropriate material or run into predators on the Web, even inadvertently. You should not underestimate the level of protection that they need.

Potential Dangers

Images, Videos, and Music

The Web has no shortage of explicit or violent images, videos, and music not suitable for children. Sites that display such media usually require membership or payment, but some do not, and those sites often display unsuitable media on their home pages.

Information

The Web is a massive storehouse of knowledge, not all of which is benign. Some site content uses profanity, and other sites offer inappropriate information on topics ranging from mixing chemicals to making weapons.

Chat Rooms

Adults who desire to meet young children often frequent Internet chat rooms. These predators disguise themselves as other children and attempt to get young participants to reveal personal details about themselves, particularly where they live or where they go to school.

Ways to Protect Children

Restrict Content

Many Web browsers have features that restrict certain types of inappropriate Web content to authorized users. These restrictions are based on ratings applied to certain sites. In Internet Explorer, click **Tools**, click **Internet Options**, and then click the **Content** tab. Use the **Parental Controls** and **Content Advisor** buttons to restrict the actions children can perform on the Web and to control the types of content they can access.

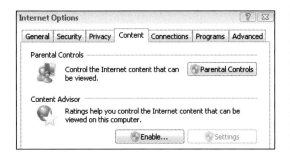

Third-Party Programs

Many third-party programs filter out content deemed objectionable for children. Among the most popular in this category are CYBERsitter (www.cybersitter.com), Net Nanny (www.netnanny.com), and CyberPatrol (www.cyberpatrol.com).

Supervision and Education

Ideally, parents should also be directly involved in protecting their children on the Web. For very young children, parents should supervise Web sessions to prevent access to inappropriate content. For older children, parents should educate them on the potential dangers and lay down ground rules for using the Web (such as not giving out personal data to strangers without permission).

Protect Your Browsing Privacy

You can protect your browsing privacy by deleting browsing history.

Every browser keeps track of a variety of data as you use the browser, such as a list of Web sites you visit. Browsers also store the data you provide whenever you complete a form on a Web site. Each browser saves to your hard drive copies of Web pages you view; these temporary files, also called *the cache*, speed up your browsing. And, each Web site you visit drops small files called *cookies* on your hard drive to store preferences, such as login information. To protect your privacy, you can delete all of this information.

Protect Your Browsing Privacy

Protect Privacy in Internet Explorer

1. Open Internet Explorer.

2. Click **Safety**.

3. Click **Delete Browsing History**.

The Delete Browsing History dialog box appears.

4. Click the boxes beside each option in the dialog box (☐ changes to ☑).

5. Click **Delete**.

Internet Explorer deletes all browsing history.

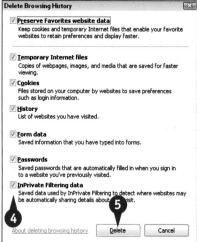

Protect Privacy in Firefox

1 Open Firefox.

2 Click **Tools**.

3 Click **Clear Recent History**.

The Clear Recent History dialog box appears.

4 Click the **Time range to clear** ⏷.

5 Click **Everything**.

6 Click the boxes beside each option in the dialog box (☐ changes to ☑).

7 Click **Clear Now**.

Firefox deletes all browsing history.

Simplify It

Can I clear browsing history in Google Chrome?
Yes. Follow these steps:

1 Click 🔧 in the upper right corner of Chrome.

2 Click **Options** to display the Google Chrome Options dialog box.

3 Click the **Under the Hood** tab.

4 Click **Clear browsing data** to display the Clear Browsing Data dialog box.

5 Click beside each item you want to clear (☐ changes to ☑).

6 Click **Clear browsing data**.

7 After Chrome clears browsing data, click **Close** twice.

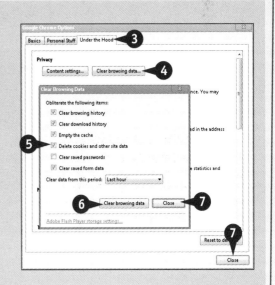

Chapter 11

Communicating Online

The Internet offers you a number of ways to communicate with other people, including e-mail messages and instant messages.

Introduction to E-Mail

E-mail is the Internet system that enables you to electronically exchange messages with other Internet users anywhere in the world. The e-mail system is nearly universal because anyone who can access the Internet has an e-mail address.

You can work with e-mail in your browser, or you can use one of the special programs available. Several of these programs are free, such as Thunderbird from Mozilla — the same company that created Firefox — and Windows Live Mail from Microsoft. Outlook, also from Microsoft, is not free, but is widely used because it combines personal information management functions with e-mail.

E-Mail Advantages

E-mail is fast; messages are generally delivered within a few minutes — sometimes a few seconds — after being sent. E-mail is convenient; you can send messages at any time of day, and your recipient does not need to be at his or her computer, or even connected to the Internet. E-mail is inexpensive; you do not have to pay to send messages, no matter where in the world you send them.

E-Mail Account

To use e-mail, you must have an e-mail account, which is usually supplied by your ISP when you open your Internet account. The account gives you an e-mail address to which others can send messages. See the section "Discover E-Mail Addresses" for more information. You can also set up Web-based e-mail accounts with services such as Hotmail at mail.live.com, Google mail at mail.google.com, and Yahoo! Mail at mail.yahoo.com. Using a Web-based account, you can send and receive messages from any computer anywhere in the world.

How E-Mail Works

When you send an e-mail message, it travels along your Internet connection and then through your ISP's *outgoing mail server*. This server routes the messages to the recipient's *incoming mail server*, which then stores the message in his or her mailbox. When the recipient checks for messages, your message is moved from the recipient's server to the recipient's computer.

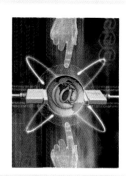

E-Mail Program

You can use an e-mail program to send and receive e-mail messages. Popular free programs include Mozilla Thunderbird and Windows Live Mail. Microsoft Outlook, although not free, is widely used; it incorporates personal information management features like a calendar with e-mail management.

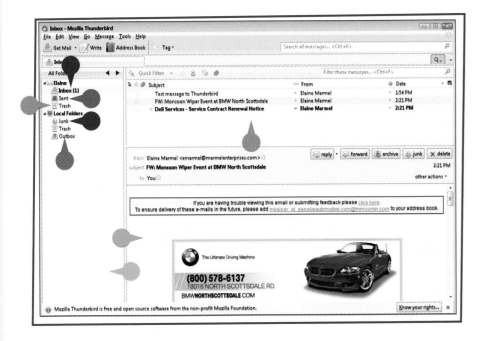

Folders Pane

This portion of the e-mail program window displays folders where the e-mail program stores various types of messages.

Inbox

This folder stores your incoming messages.

Sent Folder

This folder stores outgoing messages that you have sent.

Trash Folder

This folder stores messages that you have deleted from another folder.

Junk Folder

This folder stores messages that the e-mail program considers to be unsolicited mail.

Outbox

This folder stores outgoing messages that you have not yet sent.

Messages

This area shows a list of the messages contained in the folder selected in the left pane — in this example, the messages in the Inbox.

Message Preview

This area shows a preview of the currently selected message.

Discover E-Mail Addresses

An e-mail address is a set of characters that uniquely identifies the location of your Internet mailbox. Every e-mail address consists of three parts that you can easily identify. And, you are not limited to only one e-mail address; you can have multiple e-mail addresses.

You can send an e-mail message to another person only if you know that person's e-mail address. All e-mail programs give you the option of storing e-mail addresses — whether you use them frequently or infrequently — in an address book so that they are readily available when you need them.

Parts of an E-Mail Address

@ Symbol

The @ symbol (pronounced "at") separates the other two parts of an e-mail address: the username and the domain name. The @ symbol appears only in e-mail addresses, not in Web addresses for pages on the Internet.

Username

The username, appearing to the left of the @ symbol, is the name of the person's account assigned by the Internet Service Provider (ISP) or by the person's organization. The username is often the person's first name, last name, or a combination of both. No two people using the same ISP or within the same organization can have the same username.

Domain Name

A domain name identifies an organization on the Internet. The domain name assigned to your ISP, to your organization, or to your Web e-mail service provider appears to the right of the @ symbol in your e-mail address.

Multiple E-Mail Addresses

Most ISPs provide their customers with multiple mailboxes, each of which has its own e-mail address. Multiple mailboxes are useful if you want to provide separate addresses for each member of your family or business. You can also use multiple addresses to separate personal e-mail from e-mail for mailing lists, or when you need to provide an e-mail address at a Web site on the Internet.

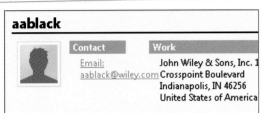

Address Book

You can use your e-mail program's address book to store the names and addresses of people with whom you frequently correspond. When you compose a message, you can then choose the recipient's name from the address book, and the program automatically adds the contact's e-mail address. This method is both faster and more accurate than typing the address manually.

Invalid Address

If you make a mistake when typing the recipient's address and then send the e-mail message, your message cannot be delivered. If you type an incorrect username or a nonexistent domain name, the message goes out, but you may receive a bounce message in return that reports delivery errors (●).

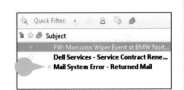

Search for an E-Mail Address

You can use one of the Internet's directory services to find a person's e-mail address. Most directory services are like the white pages telephone book and enable you to look up an e-mail address when you know the person's first and last name. You typically have to pay for these services. You can find an Internet directory service by using one of the search engines.

Compose an E-Mail Message

You can send an e-mail message to anyone whose e-mail address you know. In most cases, the message is delivered within a few minutes. You start by supplying the recipient's e-mail address and a subject. Most e-mail programs give you essentially unlimited space in which to write your message. But be concise; most people do not have the time to read long e-mail messages. Many e-mail programs provide a spell-checking feature to check your work.

You also can attach files to e-mail messages to share with the recipient. For example, you can send photos or minutes of a meeting.

Be Concise

Most of the time, e-mail contains short, to-the-point messages. This is particularly true in business, where most people use e-mail extensively. Therefore, being concise saves you time when composing a message, and it saves your recipient time when reading the message.

Check for Errors

Always thoroughly check your message for errors before you send it. Spelling mistakes, in particular, can mar an otherwise well-crafted message and obscure your meaning; many e-mail programs automatically check spelling for you. Finally, check that all your facts are accurate. Your goal should always be to write clean, clear, and correct messages.

Attachment

If you have a memo, image, or other document that you want to send to another person, you can attach the document to an e-mail message. The other person can then open the document after receiving your message. Most e-mail programs represent attachments with a paper clip (●).

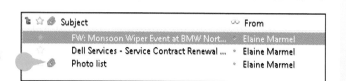

Courtesy Copy

A *courtesy copy* is a copy of a message that you send as a courtesy so that the recipient is aware of the contents of your message. In your e-mail program, you specify the main recipients in the "To" line and the courtesy copy recipients in the "Cc" line.

	To:	🔒 Juliana.Aldous@microsoft.com
	Cc:	🔒 JLefevere@wiley.com

Smileys

The subtleties of humor and sarcasm are difficult to convey in print. To help prevent misunderstandings, people often use symbols such as smileys to convey an emotion or gesture; these symbols are called *emoticons*. You create a smiley by combining a colon and a closing parenthesis. If you tilt your head to the left, this combination looks like a smiling face without a nose.

Abbreviations

To save time writing and reading e-mail, many people use abbreviations — shortened forms of common phrases — in less formal messages. Examples include AFAIK for "as far as I know," BTW for "by the way," and WRT for "with respect to."

AAMOF - as a matter of fact
B4N - bye for now
CUL8R - see you later
EOD - end of discussion
FCFS - first come, first served
GFR - grim file reaper
HSIK - how should I know

Learn About
E-Mail Etiquette

To help make e-mail a pleasant experience for you and your correspondents, you should know a few rules of e-mail etiquette. These rules are sometimes called *netiquette*, because these rules apply both to e-mail and to interactions you have on the Internet.

These rules are guidelines; the e-mail or Internet police will not come and arrest you if you break any of these rules. But the rules have evolved over time based on experience, and they have become generally accepted practices of common courtesy while working in the online world.

Do Not SHOUT

Use the normal rules of capitalization in your e-mail text. In particular, AVOID LENGTHY PASSAGES OR ENTIRE MESSAGES WRITTEN IN CAPITAL LETTERS, WHICH ARE DIFFICULT TO READ AND MAKE IT APPEAR THAT YOU ARE SHOUTING.

Use Descriptive Subject Lines

Busy e-mail readers often use a message's subject line to decide whether to read the message. This is particularly true if the recipient does not know you. Therefore, do not use subject lines that are either vague or overly general, such as "Info required" or "An e-mail message." Make your subject line descriptive enough so that the reader can tell at a glance what your message is about.

Subject: Photo list

Clarify Responses

When replying to a message, make sure that the other person knows what you are responding to by including the original message in your reply. Most e-mail programs automatically quote the entire original message when you create a reply, often highlighting with marks in the margins. If necessary, you can edit the quote to include enough of the original message to put your reply into context.

On 7/28/2010 12:24 PM, Elaine Marmel wrote:

Here's the list. Should be easy enough.

Avoid Large Attachments

Avoid sending very large file attachments. Receiving messages with large file attachments can take a long time, even with a high-speed connection. In addition, many ISPs place a limit on the size of a message's attachments, which is usually around 2MB. In general, use e-mail to send only small files.

Reply Promptly

When you receive a message in which the sender expects a reply from you, waiting too long before responding is considered impolite. Whenever possible, urgent or time-sensitive messages should be answered within a few minutes to an hour. For other correspondence, you should reply within 24 hours. If you wait too long, you can become inundated with e-mail waiting for responses.

Be Patient

E-mail is fast, but it is not meant for instantaneous communications. See the section "Communicate by Instant Messaging" for more information. Expect a message recipient to take at least 24 hours to get back to you. If you have not heard back within 48 hours, it is okay to write a short note asking the person whether your message was received.

Do Not Send Flames

If you receive a message with what appears to be a thoughtless or insulting remark, your immediate reaction might be to compose an emotionally charged, scathing reply. Such a message is called a *flame*, and it will probably only make matters worse. Allow yourself at least 24 hours to cool down before responding to the message.

Receive an E-Mail Message

Receiving e-mail is very much like getting mail through the U.S. Postal Service — often called *snail mail*. The postman delivers a letter to your mailbox, where it stays until you pick up your mail. In the same way, when someone sends you an e-mail message, it lands in your mailbox on your Internet Service Provider's incoming mail server, where it stays until you decide to check your e-mail.

To receive e-mail, you must connect to the ISP's incoming mail server to retrieve new messages into your e-mail program and proceed to handle them.

Check for New Messages

All e-mail programs have a command that you can run to check for new messages on your ISP's incoming mail server. Make sure that you are connected to the Internet before you run this command. In addition, most e-mail programs automatically check the incoming mail server for new messages.

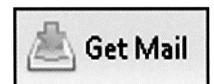

Spam and Viruses

Watches: Rolex Sport Top Product !!

watchmost@dotpiano.ru

⊘ Links and other functionality have been disabled in this m
  to the Inbox.
  This message was marked as spam using the Outlook Ju

Sent: Wed 07/28/2010 6:05 PM

Not all of the messages that you receive will come from people you know. Many unscrupulous businesses send *spam*, or unsolicited commercial e-mail. In addition, malicious users sometimes send computer viruses as e-mail attachments. Read more about spam and e-mail viruses in the sections, "Reduce E-Mail Spam" and "Guard Against E-Mail Viruses." In the meantime, do not open e-mail attachments if you are not expecting them, even if they come from someone you know.

Work with Received Messages

Store Messages

To keep your e-mail program's Inbox folder uncluttered, you can create new folders and then move messages from the Inbox to the new folders. Consider using separate folders to save related messages. For example, you could create separate folders for the subject matter of the e-mail, for projects that you are working on, and for different work departments.

Reply to a Message

When a message that you receive requires some kind of response — whether answering a question, supplying information, or providing comments or criticism — you reply to the message. You can reply only to the sender or to all recipients of the message. Do not forget to include the relevant text from the original message in your reply. Your e-mail program automatically adds "Re:" to the beginning of the subject line to indicate the message is a reply.

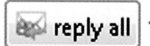

Forward a Message

If a message has information relevant to or concerns another person who did not originally receive the message, you can forward a copy of the message to that person. You can also include your own comments in the message you forward. Your e-mail program automatically adds "Fw:" to the beginning of the subject line to indicate the message is a forward.

Save or Send an Attachment

Most e-mail programs designate messages that contain attachments with a paper clip. They also use the same designator to represent the button you click to attach a file to an e-mail. Typically, to save an attachment, you can right-click the attachment and then click **Save As**. To attach a file to a message, look for a button that displays a paper clip and click it. You then navigate to the location on your hard drive where you store the file you want to attach.

Reduce E-Mail Spam

Spam is an unsolicited, commercial e-mail message that advertises anything from a baldness cure to cheap printer cartridges. Most people receive at least a few spams a day, and some people receive hundreds of them. No matter how many you receive, reducing spam can save time and reduce e-mail frustration.

Some spam is more than just annoying. For example, many spam e-mails advertise deals that are simply fraudulent. Others feature such unsavory practices as asking for money or linking to adult-oriented sites. Some spam is dangerous, linking you to sites that install spyware.

Turn On ISP Spam Filters

Many Internet Service Providers (ISPs) offer spam filtering services as part of your account. ISPs have no more use for spam than you do — spam simply makes their jobs harder because they have to deliver unwanted mail. To reduce spam, most ISPs turn on spam filtering services by default, reducing the amount of spam delivered to you. Typically, you can adjust those settings at your ISP's Web site.

Spam Blocker

> About Spam Blocker

> Manage Spam Blocker

Review Junk Mail Settings

Junk Settings

If enabled, you must first train Thunderbird to identify junk mail by using the Junk toolbar button to mark messages as junk or not. You need to identify both junk and non junk messages.

☑ Enable adaptive junk mail controls for this account

Most good e-mail programs also have junk mail filtering settings that you can adjust to help you minimize the amount of spam that actually arrives in your Inbox. In some e-mail programs, you can specify the folder where junk mail messages should appear and how often to delete junk mail. In other programs, you can set a level of filtering for the program to use to identify spam.

Do Not Respond to Spam

Never respond to spam, even to an address within the spam that claims to be a "removal" address. If you respond to the spam, all you are doing is proving that your address is legitimate.

Similarly, never click a Web site link that appears within a spam. At best, clicking the link may prove that your address is active. At worst, the link may take you to a site that displays objectionable content or that surreptitiously installs spyware on your computer.

Lose 25 lbs This Weekend!

This amazing product was developed in the secret labs of L.A. specifically for Hollywood actresses. It can be yours if you lose to be a star - and never starve yourself! Eat a cheeseburger - lose 2 lbs. Eat a whole pizza - lose 7 lbs.! The more you eat, the more you lose! It is the same A-list actresses use to lose weight for film roles, the red carpet, and beyond! Use the system the stars use for only $19.95! Order now and we'll send you our booklet, "What the Stars Know That You Don't", a valuable collection of the best skin, makeup, and fashion secrets you've GOT to know!

To be removed from this mailing list, click HERE.

Use Nicknames in Newsgroups

Harvesting e-mail addresses from posts on newsgroups is one of the most common methods that spammers use to gather addresses. Therefore, never use your actual e-mail address in a newsgroup; instead, use a nickname. Many newsgroups offer private methods of communication if you want other newsgroup users to be able to e-mail you.

Thank you for logging in, ejm123.

Click here if your browser does not automatically redirect you.

Email Address

blah@yadda.com

Use a Fake E-mail Address

When you sign up for something online, use a fake address if possible. If you must use your real address because you need or want to receive e-mail from the company, make sure that you deselect any options that ask whether you want to receive promotional offers.

Use an Alternate E-mail Address

Another way to reduce spam is to supply Web sites with an e-mail address obtained from a free Web-based account (such as a Windows Live Hotmail account or a Google Gmail account), so that any spam that you receive is sent there instead of to your main address.

Sign in with your
Google **Account**

Username: |
ex: pat@example.com

Password:

☐ Stay signed in

Sign in

Can't access your account?

Guard Against E-Mail Viruses

A computer can contract a virus that has the same basic effect on the computer that a human virus has on a person. Computer viruses are not germs, like their human counterparts. Computer viruses are malicious programs that can crash your computer or damage your files. Most viruses propagate through e-mail in the form of attachments. When you open the attachment, the virus infects your computer. You can take a few simple precautions to avoid virus infections.

Large-scale virus outbreaks occur because some viruses surreptitiously use your e-mail program and its address book to send out messages with more copies of the virus attached.

Attachments from Strangers

There is no reason why a stranger should send you an attachment. If you receive a message that has an attachment, and you do not know the sender of the message, do not open the attachment. Many ISPs want you to report this type of activity. Think of this as a neighborhood watch situation: When you do not recognize someone, you do not communicate with that person; instead, you call the police.

Attachments from Friends

If a friend unexpectedly sends you a message with an attachment, do not assume that the attachment is benign. The friend's computer may be infected with a virus that e-mails copies of itself. Send a message to your friend to confirm that he or she actually sent the file. It is always better to be safe and secure and check things out before you open unexpected attachments.

E-Mail Program Security

Most e-mail programs offer some security against viruses. For example, the program may offer to let your antivirus program analyze incoming messages to prevent viruses from being stored on your computer. Or, the program may come with a setting you can enable to prevent other programs from sending mail using your account. These options thwart those viruses that try to replicate themselves using your e-mail program.

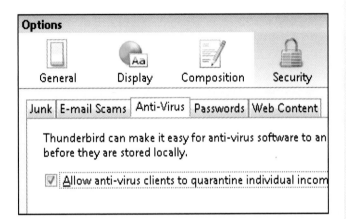

Antivirus Software

Installing a good antivirus program on your system is important, particularly a program that checks all incoming messages for viruses. Try Microsoft Security Essentials (www.microsoft.com/security_essentials), AVG (www.avg.com), or Eset NOD32 Antivirus (www.eset.com).

Read in Plain Text

The HTML message format uses the same codes that create Web pages. Therefore, just as some Web pages are unsafe, so are some e-mail messages. Those messages contain malicious scripts that run automatically when you open or even just preview the message.

You can prevent these scripts from running by changing your e-mail program settings to read all of your messages in the plain text format. You can adjust your e-mail settings in most e-mail programs, including Windows Mail, Microsoft Outlook, and OS X Mail.

Chapter 12

Wireless Computing

Many of the most common computing devices come in wireless versions, enabling you to use these devices without connecting them to your computer using cables. For example, you can purchase wireless keyboards and mice and wireless printers that you can connect to your computer without using cables.

With the appropriate wireless equipment, you can also network computers and access the Internet without cables. And, if you have the right multimedia equipment, you can stream media; for example, you can listen to music stored on your PC through your stereo system's speakers or view movies stored on your computer using your television set.

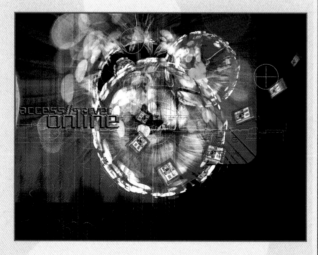

Discover Wireless Computing

Wireless computing allows you to operate your computer, communicate with others, and access resources such as a network and the Internet using equipment that does not require cables, phone lines, or any other direct, physical connection. Wireless computing devices transmit data using radio signals, and they have both advantages and disadvantages.

You will find available a variety of wireless devices, the most common being the wireless keyboard and mouse. In addition to using wireless devices, you can set up a wireless network and connect to the Internet wirelessly.

Wireless Advantages

The main advantage of wireless computing is the lack of cables, lines, and cords, which looks neater and makes devices easier to install. Wireless computing is also more flexible. For example, a wireless keyboard allows you to type a distance away from the computer; a notebook computer with a wireless network connection can usually allow you access to the network from anywhere in the same building.

Wireless Disadvantages

Wireless devices consume a great deal of power, which means that wireless peripherals require batteries, and wireless notebooks have shorter battery lives. In addition, interference from nearby devices can sometimes disrupt wireless communications, thus making them inconsistent. Finally, wireless networks are inherently less secure than wired networks, although you can take precautions to enhance security.

Radio Signals

Wireless devices transmit data and communicate with other devices using radio signals beamed from one device to another. Although these radio signals are similar to those used in commercial radio broadcasts, they operate on a different frequency.

Radio Transceiver

A radio transceiver is a device that can act as both a transmitter and a receiver of radio signals. All wireless devices that require two-way communications use a transceiver. Devices that require only one-way communications — such as a wireless keyboard or mouse — contain only a transmitter; the device you attach to your computer is a receiver.

Wireless Peripherals

You can operate your computer using wireless peripherals. To input data, you can use a wireless (often called cordless) keyboard or mouse. To output data, you can use a wireless monitor or printer.

Discover Wireless Computing *(continued)*

Wireless Networking

A wireless network is a collection of two or more computers that communicate with each other using radio signals. In an ad hoc wireless network, the computers connect directly to each other; in an infrastructure wireless network, the computers connect to each other through a common device, usually called an *access point*. Most people use a router with wireless capabilities as their access point.

Wireless Internet

Many wireless access point devices have a port to which you can connect a high-speed modem. This enables the access point to establish its own Internet connection, and nearby wireless computers can then use the Internet through the access point.

Wireless Hotspots

A wireless *hotspot* is a location that allows wireless computers to use the location's Internet connection. You can find hotspots in many airports, hotels, and even businesses such as coffee shops, restaurants, and dental offices. To locate wireless hotspots both free and pay, try using JiWire's registry of hotspots at http://v4.jiwire.com. To find free wireless hotspots, check out Wi-Fi FreeSpot at www.wififreespot.com.

The Wi-Fi-FreeSpot™
USA State-by-State li
World listed further d

In addition to the main
listing pages.

Companies (like Pane
with multiple location
site's location search
travelling.

Wireless Technologies

The most common wireless technology is Wi-Fi, a trademark of the nonprofit Wi-Fi Alliance. Wi-Fi is based on IEEE 802.11 standards. There are five main types — 802.11, 802.11a, 802.11b, 802.11g, and 802.11n — each of which has its own range and speed limits. The most common types in use are 802.11g and 802.11n. Bluetooth is another common wireless technology; using it, you can connect individual devices to automatically create ad hoc networks. Bluetooth is not commonly used in computer networks but rather to pair cell phones with cars for hands-free operation.

Wireless Ranges

All wireless devices have a maximum range beyond which they can no longer communicate with other devices. Peripherals such as keyboards have a range typically of less than 30 feet. A typical wireless router using IEEE 802.11g might have a range of 120 feet indoors and 300 feet outdoors. IEEE 802.11n can have a range of more than double its 802.11g counterpart. The frequency band that the signal uses to broadcast also affects range, with Wi-Fi in the 2.4 GHz frequency block getting a little better range than Wi-Fi in the 5 GHz frequency block.

Wireless Speeds

Wireless transmission speed — which is usually measured in megabits per second, or Mbps — is an important factor to consider when you set up a wireless network or a wireless Internet connection. Less expensive wireless networks most often use 802.11b, which has a theoretical top speed of 11 Mbps. The 802.11g standard has a theoretical speed limit of 54 Mbps. The 802.11n standard will have a theoretical speed limit of 248 Mbps.

Wireless Computing Devices

Wireless computing requires devices that have wireless capabilities. Although wireless capabilities are built in to many of today's notebook computers, for many other types of wireless computing, you need to purchase additional wireless devices relevant to the kinds of wireless computing that you want to use. You can purchase wireless input devices and wireless output devices, and, in some cases, you can give wireless functionality to devices that were built to function in a wired network.

Wireless Input

Outside of networking, the most common wireless products today are input devices, particularly the keyboard and mouse. You attach a USB transceiver to your computer, and the keyboard and mouse can operate within 20 or 30 feet of the transceiver.

Other Wireless Peripherals

Another common wireless device is a wireless print server to which you attach a regular printer; it allows all of the wired and wireless computers on your network to access the printer. Other wireless peripherals include monitors, webcams, printers, game pads, and transmitters that beam digital music from your PC to your stereo.

Wireless Handhelds

Handheld devices often have either Wi-Fi or Bluetooth wireless capabilities built in. This enables these devices to take advantage of hotspots so that you can check e-mail, surf the Web, as well as synchronize with desktop computers.

Internal Network Adaptor

To access a wireless network, your computer requires a wireless network adapter. You can open your computer case and insert a wireless network interface card (NIC) into your desktop computer so that it can connect wirelessly to your network. Older internal wireless NICs used antennas, but newer internal wireless NICs use a wire to connect to a wireless signal broadcasting device — the white box in this image — that broadcasts a signal to your wireless-capable router more reliably than an antenna. If you use a notebook computer without built-in wireless capabilities, you can insert a PC card, which truly uses no wires because the broadcasting function is built into the card.

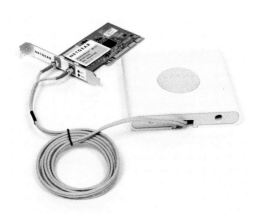

External Network Adaptor

If you prefer, you can use an external wireless network adaptor. These USB NICs are easier to install on a desktop computer because you do not need to open the computer case; instead, you simply plug this device into an available USB port. And, like PC cards, they are truly wireless because the signal broadcaster is built into the NIC.

Wireless Access Point

A *wireless access point* (AP) is a device that receives and transmits signals from wireless computers to form a wireless network. Most people use routers as their wireless access points. Most APs also accept wired connections so that you can connect both wired and wireless computers to a network. If your network has a broadband modem, you can connect the modem to the AP to enable all of the computers on the network to share Internet access.

Connect to a Wireless Network

With your wireless network adapters installed, you are ready to connect to establish an Internet connection and connect to your wireless network using a computer on the network. Most wireless routers do all the setup work for you; you simply need to plug in the router and, if you want to share an Internet connection over your network, connect your modem to your router. When you connect to a wireless network, you choose from a list of available wireless networks. You can connect to a secure network or to an available hotspot and you can disconnect from that network. You also can check your signal strength.

Establish an Internet Connection

Your computer can connect wirelessly to the Internet as well as to your local network. But high-speed modems that provide Internet access are not wireless devices. So, besides plugging the modem into an electrical outlet, you need one cable that connects your high-speed modem to the Internet port on the back of your wireless-capable router; the Internet port might be called the WAN port or the Uplink port. The router enables your computers containing wireless NICs to the share the Internet connection provided by plugging the high speed modem into the router.

Set Up the Wireless Access Point

To set up newer wireless access points — typically, a router like the Cisco Valet — you plug a USB drive that comes with the router into the first computer you want to connect to the access point, and the router software takes over, setting up the device and prompting you to enter a public name called a *Service Set Identifier* (or SSID) that identifies the network and a security password that each wireless device uses to connect to the network. You then plug the USB drive into each additional wireless device that will connect to the network to set up those devices. Older routers use a setup page that you access with your Web browser (usually at either http://192.168.1.1 or http://192.168.0.1).

Connect to a Secure Network

If the network that you want to use is unsecured — as are many public hotspots — then you can immediately access the network. However, most private wireless networks are secured against unauthorized access. In this case, the network asks you to enter the appropriate security information.

View Available Networks

After you initially set up a computer for wireless networking, or if you take your portable computer to a public place, such as a hotel, airport, or coffee shop, you can display a list of available wireless networks. In Windows 7, click the **Start** button () and then click **Connect To** (●). Or, you can right-click the **Network** icon (📶) in the Windows taskbar.

Disconnect from a Wireless Network

When you no longer need a wireless network connection, or if you want to try a different available network, you should disconnect from the current network. Display the list of available wireless networks, click the network to which you are connected, and then click **Disconnect** (●).

Reconnect to a Wireless Network

If you lose your wireless network connection or you disconnected from a wireless network that you want to use again, you must reconnect. You can right-click the **Network** icon (📶) to display the list of available wireless networks and then connect to the one that you want.

View Signal Strength

You can check the signal strength of your wireless connection. In Windows 7, click the **Network** icon (●) in the Windows taskbar to display the list of available networks. Position ⬉ over any network; a tip appears, showing the signal strength of your connection.

Wireless Network Security

Wireless network security involves implementing a few basic measures that prevent unauthorized users from accessing your network. Because wireless networks operate using radio signals that are broadcast in all directions, security becomes very important on your wireless network. To secure your network, you can use a wireless security that encrypts data so that only authorized users can read it.

Radio Signals

Wireless networks are inherently less secure than wired networks because radio signals are broadcast in all directions, including outside of your home or office. This enables a person within range to pick up those signals and access your network.

Wardriving

Wardriving is an activity where a person drives through various neighborhoods with a portable computer or set up to look for available wireless networks. If the person finds an unsecured network, he can use it for free Internet access or to cause mischief on the unsecured network with shared resources on that network. Be sure to secure your wireless network.

Open the Access Point Setup Page

On older routers, you might need to use the router's setup page to change security settings. On a computer connected to the access point, start your Web browser, type the access point address (usually either http://192.168.1.1 or http://192.168.0.1) and press **Enter**. Type the username and password (the default username and password are supplied by the access pointer manufacturer). The access point's setup page appears.

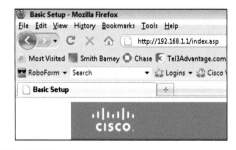

Enable WPA

Wi-Fi Protected Access (or WPA) is a wireless security feature that encrypts wireless network data so that unauthorized users cannot read it. Newer routers, like the Cisco Valet, enable security automatically during setup. On older routers, you must enable WPA using the device's setup program. Note that this setting may be called WPA Personal or WPA2 Personal.

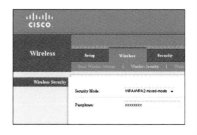

Enter a Passkey

To decrypt the data on a WPA-secured wireless network and connect to the network, users must enter a security key called a *passkey*, which is a series of characters that identifies the person as an authorized user. Newer routers prompt you to establish the passkey during setup and store the information on their USB drive; on older routers, you can use your router setup program to establish the WPA passkey you want to use. The next time you access your network, you must type the passkey. After the first time you connect to the network, Windows 7 remembers your passkey and does not prompt you for it.

Disable Broadcasting

Your operating system remembers the wireless networks to which you have successfully connected. Therefore, when all of your computers have accessed the wireless network at least once, you no longer need to broadcast the network's Service Set Identifier (SSID). As a result, you should use your router setup program to disable broadcasting and to prevent others from seeing your network. Newer routers prompt you to change the default SSID during setup; on older routers, change the name using the router's setup page.

Change Access Point Password

Any person within range of your wireless access point can open the device's setup page by entering http://192.168.1.1 or http://192.168.0.1 into a Web browser. The person must log on with a username and password, but the default logon values (usually admin) are common knowledge among wardrivers. To prevent access to the setup program, be sure to change the AP's default username and password.

Stream Media Throughout Your Home

With the right equipment, you can use your wireless network to send media — or *stream* media from your computer and play that media on other devices in your house, such as your TV or your stereo system.

To stream media, you connect to your network all devices that will use the media. You can use either a wired or wireless connection, but wireless connections are more often available on certain media-related equipment. Once all your devices are part of the network, you can use Windows Media Player to send media from any connected device to any connected device.

Setting Up the Hardware

To stream media, your computer(s) should have any edition of Windows 7 installed, and you need to set up a Home network and create a homegroup. Make sure that all your computers join the homegroup. Connect your media devices — ones that will send media to another device and ones that will receive media from another device — to the network using either an Ethernet cable or a wireless connection.

HomeGroup
Browse available libraries shared by other members of your homegroup.

 Elaine (AMD-740-5000)　　　 Elaine Marmel (AMD-740-4600)

Components and Streaming

Any computer running any edition of Windows 7 can stream media. Many newer televisions, stereo receivers, DVD players, DVRs, mobile phones, music devices like the iPod, and printers come with built-in wireless connections or Ethernet jacks. If you connect them to your network, you can stream media between all of these devices.

Digital Media Adapter

If your components do not have built-in wireless connections or Ethernet jacks, you can purchase a *digital media adapter* — a stand-alone device also called a *digital media receiver*. The digital media adapter enables you to connect your components to your network. To find playback devices that work together, visit the Digital Living Network Alliance Web site (www.dlna.org).

DLNA Certified Products

You'll find the DLNA Certified logo on all kinds of digital devices for your mobile phones, you name it. But they aren't the same TVs, PCs and m

Built to DLNA certification standards, this new generation of devices off these products to play not one but multiple roles in your digital network

DLNA Certified devices are certified in a number of different **DLNA Devi** DLNA Device Class certification that allows the product to do more thin some cases. To find *and* upload content in others. Here's a rundown of already be familiar with. See what each device can do if they are also a

Digital Media Player

To stream media, you need a software program called a *digital media player*. In Windows 7, the Windows Media Player and Windows Media Center programs act as digital media players.

Initiate Streaming

Use the digital media player that contains the content to stream media. In Windows Media Player Library mode, click the **Stream** menu (●) and click **Turn on media streaming with HomeGroup** to share your media library on the network. If you are using Windows Media Center, the content is automatically streamed.

Play the Media

In Windows Media Center, create a playlist of the media stream you want to watch or hear. Click the **Play to** menu button (●) to choose the device on your network you want to use. For example, to stream music to your stereo, create a playlist of music and then click the **Play to** button and select your stereo.

Chapter 13

Performing Computer Maintenance

You need to perform some routine maintenance chores to help keep your system running smoothly, reduce the risk of computer problems, and maintain top performance. These chores are not difficult to perform and include updating the operating system, checking for hard drive free space and errors, defragmenting the files on your hard drive, and backing up your files.

Update Your Operating System

To update your operating system, you need to download and install the latest components and programs. These updates fix problems and resolve security issues. You can reduce computer problems and maximize online safety by updating your operating system regularly.

By default, Windows downloads and installs updates every day at 3 AM or the next time you turn on your computer after 3 AM. Also by default, Windows checks for important updates, allows all user accounts on the computer to install updates, checks for updates to other Microsoft packages besides Windows, and notifies you when new Microsoft software is available.

Update Your Operating System

Check Update Settings

1. Click the **Start** button (🔘).

2. Click **Control Panel**.

   The Control Panel window appears.

3. Click **System and Security**.

   The System and Security window appears.

4. Click **Turn automatic updating on or off**.

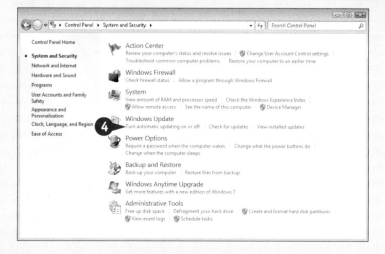

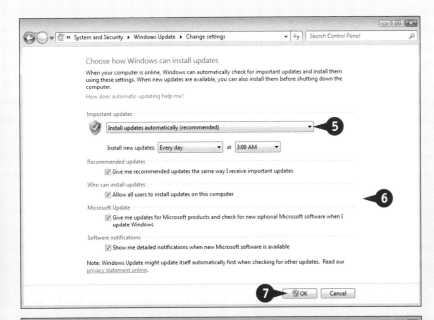

The Windows Update Change Settings window appears.

5 Click here to specify how Windows handles updates.

6 Use these options to change the updates Windows 7 downloads and who can install updates (☑ changes to ☐).

7 Click **OK**.

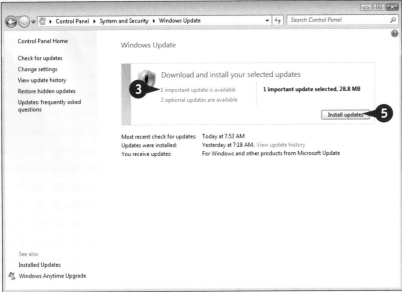

Manually Update Windows 7

1 Repeat Steps **1** to **3**.

2 In the System and Security window, click **Check for updates**.

The Windows Update window appears.

3 Click here to review and select important updates; to select an update, click ☐ beside it; ☐ changes to ☑ and click **OK**.

4 Repeat Steps **3** and **4** for optional updates.

5 Click **Install updates**.

Windows 7 downloads and installs the selected updates.

Simplify It

What are "important updates"?
Important updates include security updates, critical updates, and service packs. Security updates fix security breaches that might enable someone to infiltrate your system or infect it with a virus. Critical updates fix glitches that cause the system to behave erratically or crash. Service packs are an accumulation of updates.

What are "recommended updates" and "optional updates"?
Recommended updates generally improve your computing experience, but they do not fix anything fundamental. Optional updates are typically updated drivers and new software available from Microsoft; if your computer is working properly, you can usually skip optional updates.

Determine Hard Drive Free Space

You can check the amount of free space available on your hard drive. The amount of available free space on a drive — particularly the drive on which Windows 7 is installed — directly affects how well Windows 7 runs. If the drive's free space becomes insufficient — say, less than 20 percent of the total space on the drive — then Windows 7 may begin to run slowly and behave erratically. You might see your computer begin to freeze on a regular basis and not permit you to take any action other than to push the power button to shut off the computer.

Determine Hard Drive Free Space

1 Click the **Start** button (⊞).

2 Click **Computer**.

Note: *If Computer does not appear on the Start menu, click anywhere to close the Start menu and press ⊞ + Ⓔ.*

The Computer window appears.

3 Click the **View** button ▾.

4 Click **Tiles**.

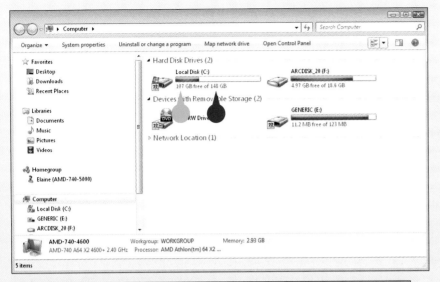

Information about each drive appears.

● This value identifies the amount of free space on the drive.

● This value identifies the size of the drive.

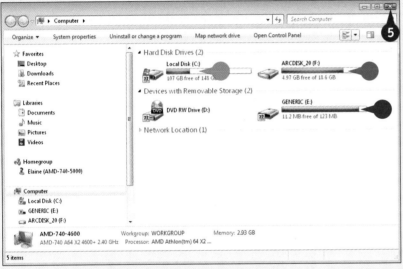

● This bar provides a visual indication of how much of the drive contains information.

● The portion of the bar representing information on the drive appears blue when the drive contains sufficient free space to add more data.

● When a drive is close to full, the bar representing information appears red.

⑤ Click ✖ to close the Computer window.

What can I do if I find that space is getting low on a drive?
You can take any of three actions:

● Delete or move files to a different drive. Media files, such as images, music, and videos take up a lot of space. See Chapter 5 for details on moving or deleting files.

● Delete programs you no longer use. To uninstall a program, see Chapter 7.

● Use the Windows Disk Cleanup program to let Windows 7 delete files it no longer uses. See "Clean Up Your Hard Drive" later in this chapter.

Check Your Hard Drive for Errors

Hard drive errors can cause files to become corrupted, which may prevent you from running a program or opening a document. Using an account with Administrator credentials, you can use the Windows 7 program Check Disk to look for and fix hard drive errors.

You should perform the hard drive check about once a week. Perform Windows 7's more thorough bad-sector check once a month. Keep in mind that the bad-sector check can take several hours, depending on the size of the drive and the frequency with which you perform this check.

Check Your Hard Drive for Errors

1 In the Computer window, click the hard drive you want to check.

Note: See the section "Determine Hard Drive Free Space" to open the Computer window.

2 Click **Properties**.

The hard drive's Properties dialog box appears.

3 Click **Tools**.

4 Click **Check now**.

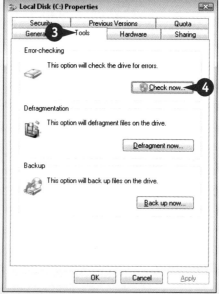

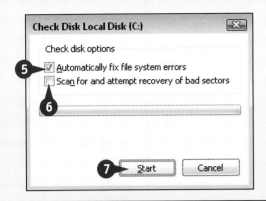

The Check Disk dialog box appears.

⑤ If you want Windows not to fix errors it finds, click here (☑ changes to ☐).

⑥ If you want Windows to look for bad sectors and attempt to recover them, click here (☐ changes to ☑).

⑦ Click **Start**.

If you are checking the drive on which Windows 7 is installed, a message appears, asking if you want the disk checked the next time you start your computer.

⑧ Click **Schedule disk check**.

The message disappears.

⑨ Click **OK**.

The next time you start your computer, Windows runs the Check Disk program and checks the hard drive you selected in Step **1** for errors.

Note: *If you did not opt to automatically fix file system errors and Check Disk finds errors, follow the on-screen instructions.*

What is a bad sector?
Your hard drive is divided into small areas called *sectors*. To avoid wasting hard drive space, Windows divides files that do not fit in a single sector and stores the parts of the files in noncontiguous sectors. A bad sector is one that — through physical damage or some other cause — the operating system can no longer be used to reliably store data.

What is a file system error?
A file system error occurs when the operating system loses track of part of a file or mixes up the parts of two or more files.

Defragment Your Hard Drive

When you *defragment* your hard drive, you reorganize it to combine the various pieces that comprise each file on the drive. Defragging makes your operating system and your programs run faster, and also makes your documents open more quickly. Using an account with Administrator credentials, you can use the Windows 7 Disk Defragmenter tool to defragment your hard drive.

You can schedule defragmentation so that you do not need to remember to do it. If your computer is not turned on at the scheduled time, Windows 7 defragments the drive the next time you turn on your computer.

Defragment Your Hard Drive

1 Click the **Start** button (⊞).

2 Click **All Programs**.

3 Click **Accessories**.

4 Click **System Tools**.

5 Click **Disk Defragmenter**.

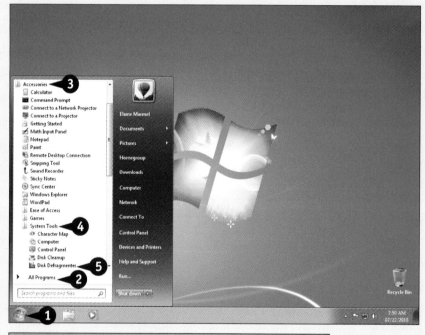

The Disk Defragmenter window appears.

6 Click **Configure schedule**.

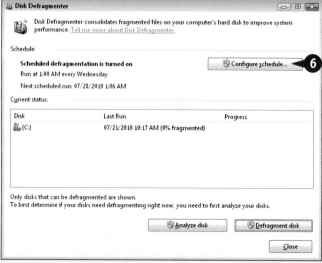

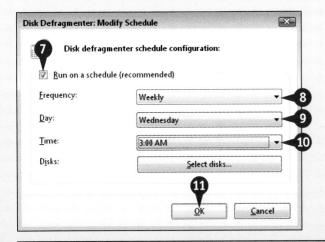

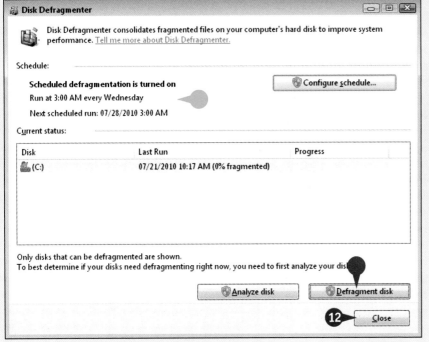

The Disk Defragmenter: Modify Schedule dialog box appears.

⑦ Click **Run on a schedule (recommended)** (☐ changes to ☑).

⑧ Click the **Frequency** ⊡ and select how often you want to defragment the drive (Daily, Weekly, or Monthly).

⑨ Click the **Day** ⊡ and select the day on which to defragment the drive.

⑩ Click the **Time** ⊡ to select the time to run Disk Defragmenter.

⑪ Click **OK**.

● The schedule you set appears here.

● If you want to defragment the drive immediately, click **Defragment disk**.

⑫ Click **Close**.

Is there a way I can tell when my drive was last defragmented?
Yes. Follow these steps:

❶ Open the Disk Defragmenter window by completing Steps **1** to **5**.

● The last time you defragmented a drive appears here, along with the amount of defragmentation.

Clean Up Your Hard Drive

You can clean up your hard drive and free up space by deleting files that your system no longer needs. If you run out of room on your hard drive, you cannot install more programs or create more documents. You can use the Windows 7 Disk Cleanup tool to clean up your hard drive and help to ensure that your system runs efficiently. The Disk Cleanup tool helps you remove downloaded program files, temporary Internet files, files in the Recycle Bin, temporary Windows files, and more.

Run the Disk Cleanup tool every two or three months or any time that your hard disk space gets low.

Clean Up Your Hard Drive

1 Click the **Start** button ().

2 Click **All Programs**.

3 Click **Accessories**.

4 Click **System Tools**.

5 Click **Disk Cleanup**.

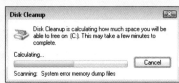

The Disk Cleanup tool calculates the amount of space you will be able to free.

Note: If your computer has more than one drive, the Drive Select dialog box appears; select the drive you want to clean up.

After calculating the space you can recover, the Disk Cleanup dialog box appears.

● This area identifies the total amount of space you can recover by selecting all file types listed in the **Files to delete** section.

⑥ Click each type of file you want to delete (☐ changes to ☑).

● This area identifies the amount of disk space you will recover based on the files you have selected to delete.

⑦ Click **OK**.

The Disk Cleanup tool displays a message, asking you to confirm that you want to delete the selected files.

⑧ Click **Delete Files**.

The Disk Cleanup tool deletes the files you selected.

Simplify It

What are the types of unnecessary files the Disk Cleanup tool removes?

Files	Description
Downloaded Program Files	Small Web page programs downloaded onto your hard drive
Temporary Internet Files	Web page copies stored on your hard drive for faster viewing
Offline Web Pages	Web page copies stored on your hard drive for offline viewing
Recycle Bin	Files that you have deleted recently
Setup Log Files	Installation files created by Windows
Temporary Files	Files used by programs to store temporary data
Thumbnails	Small versions of picture, video, and document files for display within folders
Offline Files	Local copies of network files
Per User Archived Windows Error Reporting	Files created for reporting errors and checking for solutions
System Archived Windows Error Reporting	System-created files for reporting errors and checking for solutions

Back Up Your Files

Windows 7 comes with a built-in backup program that you can use to back up your computer. You can back up your important files or create an image of your hard drive.

Because your hard drive is mechanical, it can fail. You back up so that you can recover from such a failure. To avoid losing both your data and your backups, you should store backups of your internal hard drive on an external hard drive, DVDs, or another computer on your network. The first time you back up, you establish a backup schedule; after that, Windows automatically backs up using that schedule.

Back Up Your Files

1. Click the **Start** button (🔾).

2. Click **All Programs**.

3. Click **Maintenance**.

4. Click **Backup and Restore**.

   The Backup and Restore window appears.

   Note: Be sure to connect an external drive if you intend to back up to one.

5. Click **Set up backup**.

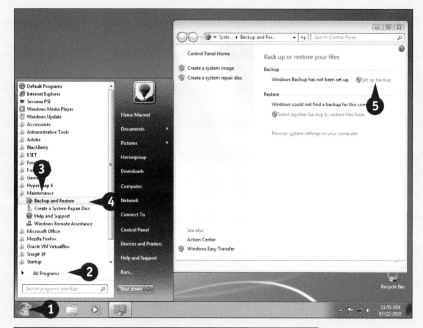

The Set Up Backup dialog box appears.

6. Click the drive where you want to store the backup.

7. Click **Next**.

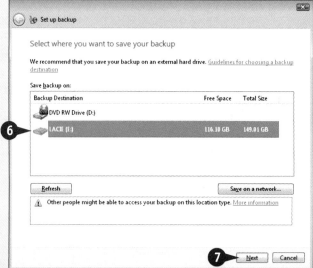

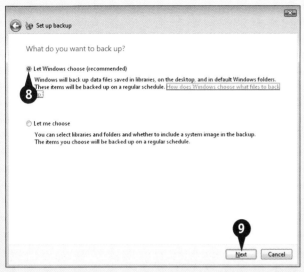

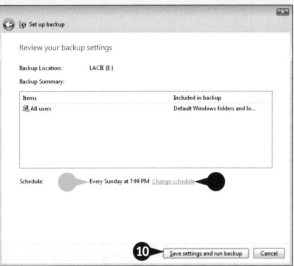

The What Do You Want To Back Up? dialog box appears.

⑧ Click **Let Windows choose (recommended)** (◎ changes to ◉).

Note: *Using this option, Windows backs up data files in libraries, on the desktop, and in the AppData, Contacts, Desktop, Downloads, Favorites, Links, Saved Games, and Searches folders for all user accounts.*

⑨ Click **Next**.

The Review Your Backup Settings dialog box appears.

● By default, Windows schedules a weekly backup.

● You can click here to change the schedule.

⑩ Click **Save settings and run backup**.

Simplify It

What is an image?
An image is an exact copy of everything on your hard drive. The image duplicates your hard drive information on a sector-by-sector basis. You cannot use a backup of important files to restore an installed program, but you can use an image.

How do I create an image?
To create an image, complete Steps **1** to **4** and then click **Create a system image** in the left pane of the Backup and Restore window. Follow the prompts on-screen. Note that you must store an image on a DVD or on an external drive.

Back Up Your Files *(continued)*

When you back up important files, Windows Backup selects files stored locally on your computer; it does not back up shared files stored on other computers in your network; Windows Backup backs up only files in libraries on your local computer.

The first time you back up your important files, you establish a backup schedule. After you complete your first backup, Windows Backup automatically backs up your important files using the schedule. If your computer is turned off when a scheduled backup should occur, Windows Backup skips the backup. Make sure your computer is on at the scheduled time or manually start a backup.

Back Up Your Files *(continued)*

Note: *If you back up to DVDs, Windows Backup prompts you to insert a blank disc. Windows formats the disc and the backup begins. Windows Backup prompts you for additional discs as needed.*

● In the Backup and Restore window, the backup progress appears here.

● The amount of available space on the backup media appears here.

● Information about the backup appears here.

⑪ Click **View Details**.

A window appears, showing the progress of the backup.

● The percent complete appears in the window title bar.

● You can click **Stop backup** if you want to cancel the backup.

Note: *Avoid canceling the first backup because you delete the schedule.*

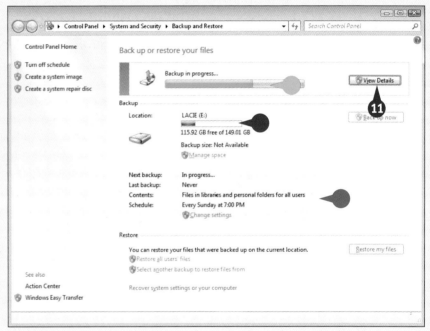

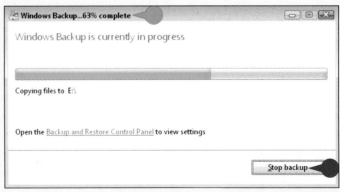

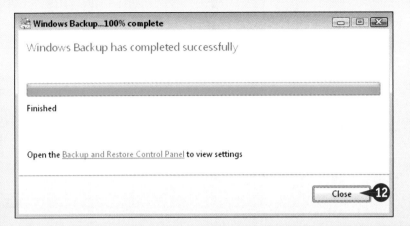

When Windows 7 finishes backing up, a window appears, indicating that the backup completed successfully.

⑫ Click **Close**.

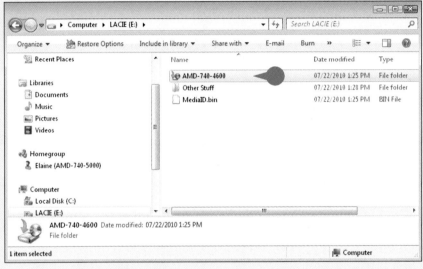

You can use Windows Explorer to view your backup file.

● Windows Backup assigns your computer's name to your backup.

Why do I see the "Other people might be able to access your backup on this location type" message when backing up to DVDs and external hard disks?
The message reminds you to keep your backups in a safe, secure location offsite, such as a fireproof bank vault. That way, your data is safe even if your computer is burned in a fire.

How do I manually create a backup?
Complete Steps **1** to **4** and, if you back up to an external drive, connect it. In the Backup and Restore window, click **Back up now**.

Restore a Backup

You can restore files from a backup of important files. You might need to restore a file if you accidentally delete it and empty the Recycle Bin before you realize you need the file. Or, you might need to restore a file if you accidentally overwrite it with another file that has the same name. And, of course, a file could become corrupt; if you backed it up before it became corrupted, you can restore it.

Keep in mind that you can restore individual files from a backup of important files, but you cannot restore individual files from a system image.

Restore a Backup

Note: *Be sure to connect an external drive or insert the first DVD of a backup.*

1 In the Backup and Restore window, click **Restore my files**.

Note: *See the section "Back Up Your Files" to open the Backup and Restore window.*

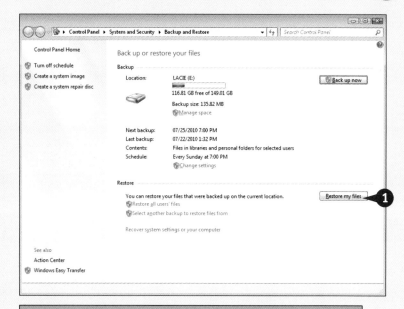

The Restore Files window appears.

2 Click **Browse for files**.

● If you want to restore an entire folder, click **Browse for folders** instead.

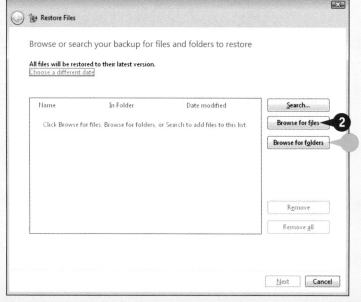

The Browse the Backup for Files dialog box appears.

③ Open the folder that contains the file you want to restore.

Note: You can click a folder in the left pane or double-click a folder in the right pane.

④ Click the file you want to restore.

⑤ Click **Add files**.

The Restore Files window reappears.

● The file you selected appears in the list.

⑥ Repeat Steps **2** to **5** to select additional files to restore.

⑦ Click **Next**.

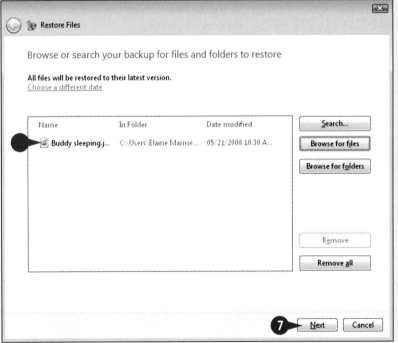

Simplify It

Can I select more than one file at a time?
Yes. In Step **4**, press and hold Ctrl as you click each file you want to restore.

What can I restore from a system image and how?
Windows Backup replaces all of your current programs, system settings, drivers, registry settings, and files with the contents of a system image. In the Backup and Restore window, click **Recover system settings or your computer**. In the Recover window, click **Advanced recovery methods** and then click **Use a system image you created earlier to recover your computer**.

Restore a
Backup *(continued)*

When you opt to restore from an important backup, you can restore a single file or multiple files. The files you restore do not need to reside in the same folder of the backup.

You also can choose, when restoring, where Windows Backup should place the restored

file(s). You can place the restored files in their original location or in a new location. And, if you opt to place them in their original location and files with their names exist at that location, you can replace the originals or you can keep both copies.

Restore a Backup *(continued)*

The Where Do You Want to Restore Your Files? dialog box appears.

⑧ Click **In the original location** (◎ changes to ◉).

● To restore to a different location, you can click **In the following location** (◎ changes to ◉) instead and then click **Browse** to select a location.

⑨ Click **Restore**.

If a file with the same name appears in the original location, the Copy File dialog box appears.

⑩ Click **Copy and Replace**.

● Alternatively, to keep the original file, click **Don't copy**.

● Or, to keep both files, click **Copy, but keep both files**.

⑪ If you want Windows Backup to handle all conflicts in the same way, click **Do this for all conflicts** (▢ changes to ☑).

Performing Computer Maintenance

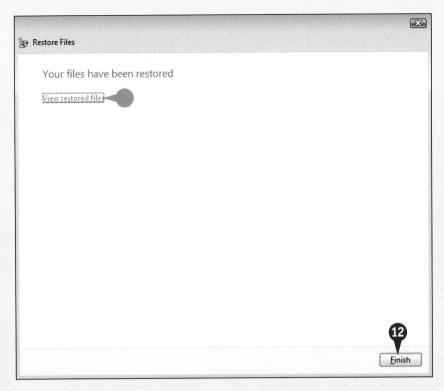

Windows Backup restores the selected files.

The Your Files Have Been Restored window appears.

● You can click here to view a list of restored files.

⑫ Click **Finish**.

Simplify It

Can I restore a file from an older backup?
Yes. Follow these steps:

① Repeat Step **1** to open the Restore Files window and click **Choose a different date**.

② In the dialog box that appears, click the **Show backups from** ⬛ to display backups from the timeframe you need.

③ Click the backup.

④ Click **OK**.

⑤ Complete the rest of the steps in this section, beginning with Step **2**.

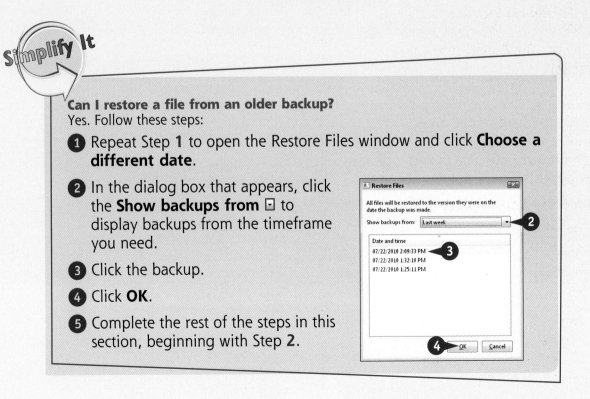

Index

Symbols and Numerics

Index

Index

Index

Index

Index